how to
remix

Printed in the UK by MPG Books Ltd, Bodmin, Cornwall

CD production and manufacture: Disctronics

Published by: Sanctuary Publishing Limited, Sanctuary House,
45-53 Sinclair Road, London W14 0NS, United Kingdom

www.sanctuarypublishing.com

ISBN: 1-86074-337-4

how to

remix

tim prochak

acknowledgements

Firstly, I'd like to thank Mark Wollascome, who is a teacher to whom books should be dedicated. He tried to teach me that a little knowledge is a dangerous thing, but unfortunately I never listened. This book is testament to my unfortunate dilettantism.

Huge thanks also to all at Ninja Tune, especially Alison, Matt, Jason and Robin. Thanks also to Time & Space, a superbly accommodating company in a cold corporate world.

Special thanks to Danny's dad, as well as my dad, too, and of course to Dan, Alice, Coop, Ruby, Greg, *et al*, to Christian for starting it all and the always wonderful Emily. Thank you.

This book couldn't have come about without Sanctuary, who thankfully didn't burn my contract when deadlines slipped.

CD contents

CD-ROM

Track 1
- MIDI files
- Samples
- VJamm video explanation
- ReadMe files

audio

Track 2
'Exo Echo' (original mix)

Track 3
'Exo Echo' (Jazzy Leanings remix)

Track 4
'Exo Echo' (White Visitation's 'Back To The Left Dub')

Track 5
'Exo Echo' (Scatty House experiment, a rough mix of a remix in progress.)

contents

introduction

I t's a bizarre concept, a book on remixing, and it's even more bizarre given the criteria. This book is part of Sanctuary Publishing's ever-expanding range of technical production manuals. But how can you teach remixing? Remixing has a kind of intangible quality found in songwriting. It's impossible to technically teach inspiration. It *is* possible to teach technique, but it is here that a quandary arises. Most producers who are going to be in the position of doing a remix will already have a thorough grasp of equipment and technique. Why, then, should there be a book on remixing?

Well, as the artists interviewed herein testify, there is a great deal more to remixing than setting a drum track to an original song. And since remixing is a relatively new idea in musical history, there are no hard rules to the process. Fortunately, this meant that I could write a book that deals with some of the ideas and concepts behind remixing, from approaches to stylistic preference – I wasn't restricted to regurgitating instruction manuals. And although there is a lot of technical information in the book, I've tried as hard as possible to include more interesting sections containing things that could almost be read with no knowledge of remixing.

Hopefully, what started as a seriously abstract concept for a book will be useful to you not only as a technical guide but also as an eclectic selection of creative ideas and opinions. On these pages are interviews with artists who, while not riding chart success all the time, are in my opinion some of the most innovative producers working in the realms of music today. And that's any music, not just dance. This is a good opportunity to restate my thanks and appreciation to all involved.

As any post-modernist will happily comment (while being careful to adopt an ironic tone), we are living in hyper-real times, times when Mickey Mouse is a person, not a trademark; times in which a W inserted neatly between a name confuses the public into thinking a change is afoot. Now, I've always been a strong believer of art reflecting the reality it exists within, and with music being the "sublime sister of painting" it should be a suitable medium in which to find the temperament of modern times. Music readily adopts a hyper-real persona. Look through any record shop and you'll find a swirling array of self-conscious borrowing, hybrids and variations on themes. Music is an ever-expanding series of permutations. But in this hyper-real time, musicians aren't restricted just to permutations of notes. (After all, there are only so many.) Today's artists can expand on a whole new level of interaction. The sound itself, production techniques and the art of synthesis open up a whole new plane for composition. Now, I'm not saying that good use of filters is the equivalent of Bach adding a sixth variation to a canon, but musicians now have a whole new digital palette with which to alter the colour and texture of sounds. Imagine if Bach had access to today's technology, if he could build his own instruments from the waveform up. I'm pretty sure he wouldn't make Europop.

As MIDI and electronic music progresses, I'm willing to hazard that so will people's opinions of what makes a good composition. Slowly people will take into account the subtle interactions and variations that occur on a processing level. Someday, someone will invent a new instrument on their home synth and it will catch on in the same way that the piano did in its first days. Someday, generic conventions will be so blurred by post-production that a new, truly original style will evolve…perhaps. But until that distant future, remixing is already bringing to the public's attention the slight change that is now occurring. Remixers use production means to change a melody into a new form. The buying public's ears are being honed to textural listening, to changes in production as well as to changes in melody. And we have the technology…

The mentality of remixing being just reworking the same tune but faster is slowly disappearing, and as home production becomes more widespread so bedroom remixing will be sure to follow. The white-label market is already swamped with illegitimate remixes made by bored producers, some of which override copyright and find their way into the mainstream. The aim of this book is to equip those bedroom-inhabiting masses with the framework to start mashing up other people's material, although of course the same techniques can be applied to using samples or even to standard songwriting. As I will monotonously stress throughout this book, there are no rules.

chapter 1

welcome to remix world

"Without music, life would be an error."
    Friedrich Nietzsche

"Without music to decorate it, time is just a bunch of boring production deadlines or dates by which bills must be paid."
    Frank Zappa

Stop. Listen to the air. Define the random clicks of sound waves into a pleasant, easy-access generic style. Done? Good. I think you'll find that the air nowadays runs to the trend of breakbeat, no-wave garage. Listen again. That's the sound of a rabid, aging journalist investing his last pennies on an ironic Prada single glove. Why? He unwittingly told himself to do so two weeks ago. The sound of the heavy air around your head is the future. A paranoid psychic told me so.

But the present – yep, now, this very second – is dominated by dance music and its unholy brethren of variations. From this hack's vantage, you could almost say that dance music is born in the post-modern goo of remixing. What is house? Not the placement of four-to-the-floor beats over obscure '60s electronica and '70s disco? Perhaps. Is big beat just a revamping of everybody's favourite, rock 'n' roll? I couldn't say. Drum and bass, jazz and death metal with faster Motown beats? No. Nope. No sir. The present is certainly dance, and dance is certainly a hybrid of many styles. And what is a hybrid but a random form of a remix? But, since the issue of time has been raised, a little context seems necessary.

history, or the lineage of unoriginality

It's hard to place the exact temporal invention of remixing. One could say that a minor fugal variation by an admiring composer constitutes a remix, but tracing roots away from a tree only leads to more that you can't see, as many professional DJs never say.

Roots, however, are the most logical place to start – dub roots, that is. The word *dub* is now used throughout the world of dance music to describe a remix, a dub plate (ie a single or limited-number vinyl pressing) or, for that matter, a bass-heavy song, but primarily it's a remix. Why? Because dub reggae artists began the trend we now call remixing as far back as the '60s, initially in the quest for sound-system exclusivity, but later as a way of re-using already recorded rhythm tracks.

The history of dub in Jamaica can be seen as an evolution in three phases. Firstly, there were instrumentals, songs that had their vocal lines taken off at a second pressing, which was effectively a remix, in that it was recognisable as the original and yet different. Secondly, "versions" began to appear, songs to which the studio engineer added material, such as effects or extra parts. These emerged at around the end of 1968, appearing on the B-sides of most Jamaican singles. Thirdly, dub arrived in the familiar sense of radically remixed tracks in 1972, accredited largely to Osbourne Ruddock, aka King Tubby. These dub pioneers have influenced modern dance stylistically as well as in attitude. Not only will you find dub atmospheres nestling alongside cheesy synth lines, but the whole idea of cutting up an independent song with a clear juxtaposition was born from artists like King Tubby.

dancing in the living room

Meanwhile, across the Atlantic, disco was spawning another ungodly coke-fuelled style of music. Everyone's favourite introduction to drum programming, house, was being born. House music is a continuation of disco. We're not talking disco as defined by groups like The Bee Gees or the *Saturday Night Fever* bubblegum that led to the popular '70s slogan "disco sucks"; instead, we're talking about classic black, urban, Philadelphia, R&B-style disco, as first defined by artists like First Choice, Loletta Halloway, Barbara Roy and MFSB. In fact, many consider the drum patterns used in MFSB's classic 'Love Is The Message' to be a primary building block in house music. (Now consider the debate on originality, where remixes begin and originals end.) This particular track has been remade and remixed many times – and, indeed, will continue to be for the rest of the century, if you consider a drum pattern to be a building block for a remix.

House music's origins stretch back to 1977, when New York DJ Frankie Knuckles came to Chicago to establish an after-hours dance club called the Warehouse (house, get it?). Knuckles drew large crowds because he successfully incorporated popular New York-style mixing and remixing techniques with black urban disco, which incidentally were inherited from Jamaica. The early house grooves were characterised by a raw, steady beat (four to the floor, yes indeed), piano riffs and haunting, synthesised tremblings, borrowing roots from a lot of avant-garde electronica and ambient music, such as German synth pop and Sakamoto.

Over the years, house music grew, splintered off and incorporated other musical styles, much in the same way that hip-hop did. Both of these genres are intimately linked with the idea of remixing. (Grandmaster Flash's 'Rapper's Delight' is essentially a remix of the disco tune 'Good Rhymes'.) Hip-hop is rooted in the cut-and-splice ideal, originally relying on borrowing bits of music and rearranging them, either via decks or by manually splicing and sticking together audio tape. (Parallels can be drawn to the *musique concrète* movement, but I won't draw them.) This reassembly of source material is what we now know as remixing, although that isn't to say that hip-hop wasn't a truly original concept.

Back to the evolution of house. In 1984 and 1985, Chicago house migrated to New York, where it was integrated with the city's fully produced club music and given better arrangements, better orchestration and powerful, gospel-like vocals. The continuing integration (or hybridisation, itself a watchword in recent musical trends) of Chicago house and New York-style R&B club music eventually led to what we now call deep house and garage – American garage, that is, not its UK counterpart, although you can argue that it shares a similar lineage. Tracks with soulful, gospel-like vocals are often classed as garage, a genre named after the famed but now-defunct New York house club of the same name. (You'll see that a pattern seems to be emerging, with styles imaginatively being named after the clubs that championed them.)

In 1989, this music arrived in Belgium, where at that moment a real new-beat rage was going on. Soon after that, Belgian DJs started mixing this new beat with some house – live remixing, if you will. It became seriously popular. Clubs like Boccaccio, Barocci and La Rocca filled up and new clubs were opened. As is the case with any underground-based music, house began to find itself within the commercial ranks. Some of its pioneers, like the group JM Silk, signed major-label recording contracts, while pop stars like Rick Astley and Natalie Cole latched onto the house groove, again a tentative nod towards the changing and hybridising nature of music. This commercialisation was shunned by the core house audience and resulted in some of its originators going further underground and emerging with new forms of house. Acid house, a hybrid (that word again) of traditional and hi-NRG dance music, was one example. This genre was characterised by a bumblebee-like bass line, known as the "funky worm" (clearly). The funky worm was created by using the now-classic TB 303 synthesiser, recaptured in all its analogue charm in Roland's Groovebox.

Interestingly, the term "acid" initially referred to burning someone by sampling or "biting" someone's musical style, a concept that fits nicely with the process of remixing. This translation was lost when the music travelled overseas to London, where house fans imbued the term with the '60s' drug connotation. (Don't quote me on this as, with everything acid house, you really did have to be there.) It was here that house began to fuse with forms of electro and industrial music, and it was this fusion that laid some of the groundwork for the current rave and techno scenes, along with probably all the styles of dance music you've ever encountered.

Simultaneously, back across the Atlantic, traditional house was beginning to fuse with hip-hop, thanks to Brooklyn-based producer Todd Terry and Chicago house veterans Fast Eddie and Tyree. Prior to this, hip-hop and house were on opposite sides of the musical spectrum. All that changed, however, when Rob Base and EZ Rock dropped the classic jam 'It Takes Two'. The funky, Motown-style beat shaped what we now lovingly call breakbeat, and it somehow managed to unite the two camps. Its existence helped to make Terry's house style more palatable for the traditional house audience. Prior to this, Terry's grooves – which were characterised by classical piano riffs, skilful sampling and mid- to up-tempo hip-hop beats – were at home among those into the Latino freestyle. (Note how the last sentence includes three generic styles, and even more, if you consider its roots. The mixing of styles equals new styles, you see? Of course, it's easy now to say "remix".)

In Chicago, the tracks produced by Fast Eddie and Tyree seemed to be more rooted in traditional house, with a rap now being incorporated. Eddie's Planet Rock-like groove 'Yo Yo Get Funky' is a classic, and many credit him with coming up with the term "hip-house", although hopefully you don't care about his semantic inventions. Meanwhile, as hip-house was taking hold, techno house was being born in Detroit. Folks like Kevin Saunderson, Juan Atkins and Frankie Bones are the primary names that are associated with the rise of this genre. The techno style produced by Saunderson came in the form of the group Inner City and was by nature a fully produced or deep house with a slightly hard, electronic edge, while Juan Atkins and Frankie Bones' grooves seemed to have more of an electronic, metallic, industrial sound.

As house advanced and its various genres and sub-genres began to fuse with other musical styles, the groundwork was being laid for the current techno scene. All of this twisting and spluttering of musical styles helped to produce all that we now hold familiar in dance music Where would civilisation be without FSOL's 'Papua New Guinea' or 'Three Blind Mice' or 'Renegade' or 'Helicopter' or 'GO' or… The list is endless and, of course, is governed by personal preference. The major point, however, is that remixing is an inherent element of dance music. It has existed from the beginning, and some would even go as far as to say that dance music was born out of remixing.

pre-history

"Ultimately, remixing is as old as the record industry. The first time Stravinsky walked into a studio, he found a guy in the control room who was introduced as 'the producer who [was] going to fix it'. If the industry can do that to Stravinsky, who the hell are any of us to complain?"
    The Rapino Brothers

Musique Concrète

Musique concrète was a style of music (in its loosest possible sense) that was developed by a group of musicians in Paris in around the late 1950s. Tied in with the Dadaist movement, they made recordings that were essentially sonic montages, utilising existing acoustic phenomena – bells, railway noises, fragments of human speech, animal noises etc. These elements were recorded, manipulated and put together in startling patterns. This random soundscaping was rooted strongly in Dadaism, but ideology doesn't concern us. *Musique concrète* can be seen as the birth of creative sampling and a definite cousin of remixing. (It also foretold many ambient journeys that appeared in the early '90s.) Its proponents rearranged natural sounds into a semblance of order, and this form of rearrangement is still with us today. In fact, audio manipulation and nods towards Dadaism have recently re-entered the public sphere with the increasing popularity of labels like Warp, Ninja Tune and Leaf Recordings.

Instant Classics And Musical Offerings

In another remix offshoot, it was often common practice for classical composers to take themes and sometimes whole segments of compositions and rework them into their own pieces. A famous example of classical remixing comes from Frederick the Great's meeting with Johann Sebastian Bach. The King of Prussia was a serious lover of music and one of the first patrons to recognise the virtues of the newly developed "piano forte" (well, it was the 1700s), or what we now know as an honest-to-goodness piano. Frederick not only admired pianos and played music but also had a particular soft spot for muso golden boy Bach. He held regular musical evenings at which he and famous composers would play. On one evening, Bach arrived unannounced to one of these *soirées*. Taken aback, the King showed the composer around, insisting that he played the brand-new piano fortes. Bach was famed for his ability to compose on the spot, and he asked the King for a theme. Frederick duly played him one of his compositions and Bach immediately created a canon (a number of variations on a single phrase) on it. Indeed, the King was very pleased by Bach's visit, although he was happier still a few month later when he received, in notation, six variations of his original theme, penned by Bach, under the title 'A Musical Offering'. Could Bach have been the godfather of remixing?

While we've seen its growth inside the dance machine and in historical instances, the word "remix" remains just that, a word. We still lack a serious definition for it, and this eases us smoothly into the next chapter…

chapter 2

semiotics and the remix

"Call me a cab!" "OK, you're a cab."
The Marx Brothers.

what is a remix?

This question rates high up there with many deep philosophical inquiries, such as, Why are we here? Is there a mind/body dualism? And why are The Spice Girls still releasing records? All of these questions have thousands of answers but no satisfactory, conclusive solution. It calls to mind the Kruder And Dorfmeister "mix" of 'Transfatty Acid' by Lamb, first brought to my attention through a friend, whose friend had taped him some DJ mix on an unlabelled, poorly recorded tape. Many unknown and forever unnamed tunes were also on this tape, one of which was the K&D mix of 'Transfatty Acid'. We loved it, designed as it was for the most brutal of comedowns, so logically we tried to find out what it was on recognising the singer as "that bird from Lamb". We bought album after album and finally found it, but, shock of shocks, the lush, hard-attack organ and jazzy staccato beats were replaced by a sparse drum track and some vocals. The version we had was a remix. But for all that we were concerned, the version we had was the original (and, for that matter, much better).

So, is an original merely in the ear of the beholder? Where is the line between an original and a remix? A better illustration would be Norman Cook's reworking of Cornershop's 'Brimful Of Asha'. The chances are that the average music-buying public have never heard the original, but that didn't stop a remix from reaching Number One. To an extent, this holds true of most of Fatboy Slim's other single successes. 'Praise You' is basically the R&B tune 'Praise You' minus the rest of the song plus a breakbeat and some of those Ferrero Roche synth sounds (ie "With this cheap tinniness you are really spoiling us").

The idea of the new and improved version is something inherent in dance music. Take the re-release of 'It's Not Over Yet', 'Bullet In The Gun 2000' and 'Binary Fineries 1998', becoming '1999'. Some people would argue that the whole existence of remixing, re-doing and re-releasing is just rehashing old ideas and is illustrative of music's present quagmire, that nothing new can exist so constant hybrids are created, giving the illusion of "new", and as the circle tightens from week to week the only future is the sampling of last week's Number One with a ridiculous, new and improved beat. This cynical view is countered by those who see diversity as post-modernity's glorious child. Instead of simulacra and illusion, music is a melting pot of reflexivity, self-referencing and general hope. Music can progress because its proponents are aware of its lineage. Musicians know what has gone before, which allows them to create new and exciting songs in a mix of available styles. The palette is either growing or becoming muddied, depending on which boat you're sitting in. DJs themselves can be seen in this light. They play other people's music, adding their own flair style and effects, and achieve love, fame and money in the process. (Sound familiar? Not the love, fame and money bit, but the practice of adding to other people's original music.) DJs are sat firmly in the same post-modern boat as remixes and dance music itself.

So, we've determined that remixing can be viewed in at least two lights without drawing any definite conclusions, and that you can definitely get away with calling it post-modern. Still, what *is* a remix? Put simply, with no reading between the lines, it's a "version" that is an interpretation of another song, recognisable as the other song but still markedly different, and that's how remixing is different from the rest of dance music. Although dance samples other material left, right and everywhere, it usually does its best to conceal its sources. A remix, by default, pays homage to its original source.

Thunderprow

Time now for a diversion. Think of this section as a metaphor for this chapter. The Greeks were famed for their ship-building skills. They built special ships with reinforced hulls that were capable of ramming other ships and sustaining very little damage. One particular boat built in this style was called the *Thunderprow*, and it was so strong that people said it had been blessed by the gods. Having made several successful raids and voyages, the ship had come back to port for repairs to its prow. In fact, it needed such extensive repairs that almost half of its timbers had to be replaced. Because of the esteem in which the craft was held (after all, it *was* blessed by the gods themselves), the old timbers were kept, even down to the original nails – now bent and rusty – and stored by the proud citizens with a view to making a sculpture some day as a tribute.

The next year saw *Thunderprow* in more exploits and in need of more repairs. This time, it needed another third of its timbers replaced, although it was noted that none of the new timbers had suffered. In fact, in the following year, it became apparent that the old timbers weren't really taking the strain as well as the new ones. The captain, who's name was Sorties, ordered her back to the boatyard, where he ordered that all of the remaining original timbers had to be replaced, and to complete the job he also ordered new sails and fittings so that the boat would be ultra-presentable for the forthcoming boat show. As before, the old parts were stored carefully, but this time a strange thing happened. Whilst *Thunderprow* was out attacking enemy ships, the people of the port carefully rebuilt the ship using all of the collected original parts, not as a warship – the bits were too damaged for that – but as a land monument to their crowning naval achievement.

When *Thunderprow* returned from battle, it was in disgrace. Time after time at sea, it had missed ships that it had been attempting to ram, or had caused insufficient damage. In one case, it had even snapped off its famous prow on an enemy that suffered virtually no damage. When Sorties and his battle-weary crew returned to port, they were shocked to see another boat with a specially reinforced hull sitting on trestles. The only difference between this ship and their beloved *Thunderprow* was a plaque inviting the public to come on board "the original *Thunderprow*". Sorties was seriously pissed off by this and began to shout profanities at everyone: "By building this boat, our boat has ceased to be *Thunderprow*, and now the only boat blessed by the gods is a heap of junk sitting on dry land."

Surprised at Sorties' outburst, the townsfolk insisted that this couldn't possibly be the case. Why, there was no question that the captain's boat had definitely been the original *Thunderprow* after the first refit, and indeed it was still the only *Thunderprow* after the second refit. The third therefore could not have affected its authenticity. Was he seriously suggesting that pulling out the last original nail had suddenly ceased to make it the real *Thunderprow*? Anyway, if there really was an original *Thunderprow*, it wasn't an earthly one but a mental idea in the mind of the designer. Sorties thought that this was absurd and insisted on the model ship being dismantled and burned. This was done, but it didn't help *Thunderprow*'s poor performance, and people even muttered that the captain had burned the only Greek warship blessed with the invincibility of the gods.

So, which ship was the original *Thunderprow*? Does such a thing as an original truly exist, except in some abstracted thought form? And does it matter at all to someone who wants to get into remixing? Well, again, it all boils down to which boat you're sitting in. One of the most important parts of remixing is to *know the original*. Listen to it inside out, upside down, over breakfast and as you sleep, until subliminal dreams make your ears bleed and all you're capable of doing is reciting S-Club 7 lyrics and reading a letter you once wrote to your parents after a particularly heavy weekend. Think of Sorties' boat as your remix. How much can you take away and change before it starts being an original composition in itself? What traits – hook, feel or melody – lie at the heart of the original song? Take them and exploit them with no care for post-modern beginnings or endings.

The only trouble with the above metaphor is that you're now left with an even vaguer idea of the terms "original" and "remix". This is a good thing for producers and musicians but a bad thing when it comes to explaining to loved ones why that Photek version isn't a different song, just a different version, and why you're sitting there with some other people's folk recordings and trying to rework them into this year's Balearic chart-topper. So, again, what is a remix? Nothing, apparently. Just the evolution of an idea.

"Remixing in its purest form is, to me, about hearing a song and needing to respond to it. There is something in the vocal tune, something in the words, that kicks your mind off thinking of harmonies and variations. Then you wonder what that line would sound like with a major chord under it rather than a minor one. Then you start to hear a double-time or half-time beat under it. The feeling is the same as the original, yet at the same time it's worlds away. That's because it's one person's take on another person's creation."
    Gavo

"Remixing is just retelling the story with different characters."
    William Orbit

chapter 3

validity and artistic principle

*"Remixing is about the marketing tail wagging the dog. We don't get
involved in that because it's horrible and formulated and for people who
have no self-belief."*
        Morcheeba (you may remember their appearance on a car advert)

remixing as an art form

For some time, there has been a cadre of musicians who frown on
remixing, regarding it as proof of an artist's incapability of being original,
even going as far as to call it talentless theft. I think that this stems from
an interesting trait in music-making. It's a strange occurrence that music
seems to be the only medium of expression that openly encourages
reinterpretation. I have trouble imagining Faber & Faber ringing up Jilly
Cooper to ask for a remix of 'The Wasteland' – "We want an upbeat
version so that it reaches a wider audience." No, I doubt very much that
Eliot would stand up for a remix treatment, even if his publishers got
Moby to do stanza 14.

The same applies to art, the most recent Turner prizewinner
notwithstanding. Tracy Emin is yet to remix the old masters and, as far as
I can remember, Picasso never got a down-with-the-kids upstart to
sample Guernica. Why, then, has remixing become the acceptable face of
today's music? I like to think that it shows the medium's ability to adapt
and, to an extent, music's honesty. Someone remixes another's song and
it's no big deal. Art, literature and film "pay homage" and the same
applies to music (although these fields are self-styled, high expression,
while music is just popular). Those who frown upon remixing tend to
regard music as being deservedly part of "highbrow" expression.
Honesty about influence isn't overt in art, unlike remixes in music.

Clearly, then, it's remixes that make music fall into popular expression and enrage the disbelievers.

So, are remixes valid? Well, producers everywhere will argue this one. Some (usually R&B stars) insist that what they do is the divine action of God, and that to remix God would be sacrilegious. Others simply shake their heads and grin.

If you regard an original song as a landscape or an object to be painted, each painter will interpret the view differently, adding his own mark to the scene, changing the light, etc. A great painter will record truth through his own eyes, while a great painting is both a record of a scene and a personal vision. In the same way, a good remix is a personal interpretation of an already existing song. It is both the original and something more. I tend to share the view expressed by the Dreem Team in a recent interview: "People should start to think about calling it reworking or re-producing. The days of simply adding a beat to someone else's work are long gone." In this sense, it's easy to draw parallels. I'm not entirely committed to the idea myself, but it can never be said that remixing is a blag for those who don't have the talent to write their own songs. It takes great skill and a good deal of technical and musical knowledge to create worthy remixes. (Refer to the section on "*Musique Concrète*" for further artistic back-up.)

how to retain integrity or pander to the artiste

This is a strange one. Saying that integrity is achieved through originality is all well and good, but remixing relies on taking its inspiration from already recorded songs. A remix with artistic integrity stands alone yet bears a clear family resemblance to its predecessor. How can you satisfactorily take and still be original?

Talent and creativity play a large role. Some good practices to follow, however, are to sample sparingly but effectively and develop an ear for central melodies, although this doesn't always mean to sample the main hook. Listeners have a wonderful talent for inserting melodies, so just hinting at a phrase can sometimes work. There is no step-by-step guide to validity, so it pays to experiment. More about retaining the elements of an original is covered later, but for now bear in mind that not all commissions require art or, for that matter, quality. Bad remixes are unfortunately a by-product of the money-inspired record industry.

It's worth paying particular attention to the section written with Jason

Swinscoe later in the book. As someone who could well make a bad song into a genius remix, the advice that he offers here is probably the best around.

chapter 4

getting started

"Imposition of order must equal escalation of chaos."
The Law of Entropy

setting up

It's basic, I know, but it's definitely a requirement: in order to remix you'll need some equipment. However, while what's listed below is the system I'm using to write this book, you'll need most or, preferably, all of the equipment mentioned here. The studio set-up I use is a far cry from that employed by professional studios, so you should easily be able to replicate it. One biggish remix will pay for all you'll need and more.

I currently use a G4 Mac running Cubase VST version 5.0 with a Delta 66 audio card and an Omni I/O box. I also have Steinberg's ReCycle and Peak. Outboard, I've got a Yamaha A5000 linked to a Roland SoundCanvas. Occasionally, I use a Groovebox, but usually just for its arpeggiator, as all of its sound banks have been sampled. For a professional remix – or, for that matter, for a professional song – all that an avid producer needs is a computer with a MIDI sequencer and a sampler. (Actually, the sampler is optional, but I wouldn't swap mine for the world.) Nice extras include a semi-decent microphone and some form of outboard effect, purely to conserve memory.

You'll need a sampler to carry out all of the workthroughs and exercises in this book, but most of the exercises can be adapted to an audio-enabled sequencer. (Cubase and Logic Platinum can happily deal with loop-editing and mangling.) So, in the best possible *Blue Peter* style, to remix you'll need a computer, a sequencing program, a sampler and some form of MIDI keyboard to trigger it.

what to buy

Where do you start if you want to invest in a home studio? The present market is swamped with competitors all offering apparently similar products.

Mac Or PC?

Realistically, you'll be choosing between an Apple Macintosh and a PC. (Only the very rich invest in supercomputers, and Atari STs aren't as prevalent as they once were.) So, which brand is for you? In my opinion, always go for the Mac. If you've never used a computer before, the Mac's operating system is logical and easy to follow, nudging you gently towards its use, and it also comes equipped to handle audio. The G3 iMac models also make you feel as though you're in *The Jetsons*, which is either a good or a bad thing, depending on your penchant for animated futurism. The major drawback with Macs, however, is their price. You'll generally find it easier to find a cheap PC bundle package from a warehouse than an inexpensive iMac. Having said this, however, if you choose a PC, you'll definitely require a soundcard, which will be an extra couple of hundred pounds. Add a MIDI converter and relevant software to that and you're very rapidly entering a similar price band. On the whole, PCs are more numerous, being the bulk buy of businesses and schools, so user help may be easier to find. Ultimately, of course, the choice is one of personal preference. Mine happens to be for the Mac, especially when using audio. The reasons for this are simple:

- Macs have a fully customisable OS (Operating System). If you don't need your Internet, File Sharing or ColorSync control panels running, you can disable them, freeing up resources and system memory. There's no need to run a bunch of extensions which are never used. You can always switch between different configurations;

- Macs come equipped with reliable hardware, built by Apple and only by Apple, providing good compatibility and making it easier to install extra hardware;

- PC compatibility – you can read, write and format PC floppies, CDs, zips, etc;

- Macs can be booted from a CD. If something happens to the OS or the hard disk and it doesn't boot up properly any more, you can boot up by using your system disk or an application like Norton System Tools to fix what's broken;

- Easy installation of programs. There are no DLLs or VBXs. Simply delete the folder and the program is gone;

- Average ease of use. Microsoft can be accused of borrowing from Apple in the new version of Windows;

- Macs are much more stable than PCs;

- Macs have native processor support. What's the use of a 32-bit processor if you have to go through an eight-bit bottleneck? G4s are now running on 128-bit processors, just like high-end sequencers.

which sequencer?

If you've got a computer set up, the next question you might ask is, Which sequencer is the best? The answer, again, is one of personal preference. At the present time, there are three major pieces of software available.

Pro Tools

There seems to be sort of Pro Tools elitism that exists in the realm of home recording, as it's the most hacked of all of the available music programs. So why the interest? The program was designed with film scorers in mind and offers minute manipulation and seriously crisp recording for Hollywood composers. At first, it was purely an audio program, but recently a high-end MIDI sequencer has been added. Being fully automated, it's the popular choice of live dance acts that use sequencers onstage, so the "pro" in Pro Tools is apparently not just a clever name. However, the pricing reflects its reputation, and at the time of writing it's the most expensive sequencing program available.

Cubase VST

Cubase is a name that invokes burnt images of unpopular teenagers with misappropriated Ataris churning out happy hardcore for major labels. Certainly the bedrooms were semen-stained effigies of acid house, but the program was a testament to the potential of individual perseverance. Synonymous with MIDI sequencing, Cubase is the most popular music program available. You can get it in a number of forms and versions, and it tends to reside in a medium-to-high price range. It's my program of choice, and I personally think that the results achieved in Pro Tools can be easily replicated in Cubase with just a little bit of extra sweat.

Logic

Available in three different precious metals, Logic caters to all strata of the sequencer market. Offering a very similar platform to Cubase, it can be bought (in its least valuable metal) more cheaply than the other three. And remember, you can always sequence on a four-track machine, with a bit of experimentation.

Sharing its birthplace with Cubase (Germany) isn't the only similarity, either; Logic also includes VST compatibility, like the other sequencing programs, and divides audio and MIDI in the same way as its Steinberg competitor. However, its main claim to fame is its resistance to MIDI latency. Logic users (lines were drawn early on, and most producers rabidly stand by their choice of program) will often cite its low latency, although a millisecond added to a bar – inaudible to most – seems fairly negligible in real life.

Your choice of sequencer will be made primarily with respect of price. Remember that all do a very similar job, and that the real factor will be your preference of operating system. If money is no object, you can try all three, but Cubase or Logic seem to be the programs of choice.

However, the big three aren't the only options. Vision, Mixman and even EJay offer usable sequencers for musicians on tighter budgets. You can also bypass the whole software route by buying a hardware sequencer or a phrase sampler. This opens up a whole new set of byways and country lanes, roads far too long to explore now. The advantages accorded by software are price and versatility, boons not always catered for by hardware.

samplers

Things become complicated now. With most of the major synth manufacturers producing their own models, it's first necessary to select a brand and then try to deal with an ever-increasing series of numbers that follow a seemingly random order. Brand loyalty is as fierce in buying samplers as it is in choosing sequencers. When buying, try out as many different machines as possible. Because producer A is just as right as producer B, the only way that you'll be able to truly find out which is best for you is to try out both of their recommendations. For personal reference, the sampling world is laid out like this.

Akai

Akai is for sampling what Cubase is for sequencing. Their S range of samplers is something of an industry standard, and these models are renowned for their easy operating systems and huge sample libraries. In the same way that Craig David won Best Hair at the *Smash Hits* poll-winners' party, Akai became the studio favourite purely on popular opinion and hearsay. But, as with hair awards, the majority isn't always right. Akai fall down in three major areas:

- Affordability – Although entry-level samplers can be picked up very cheaply, a top-of-the-range Akai will require a serious investment;

- Effects – Akai have never offered a huge amount of choice for effects junkies. Indeed, some of their samplers offer no effects board at all;

- Manipulation – The other major downfall is the limited beat and audio manipulation offered by Akai samplers. Filters and remix functions are all better catered for by other manufacturers.

Yamaha

Quite new to the sampler market, Yamaha offer three main studio samplers: the A3000, the A4000 and the A5000. With the launch of the A3000 a few years ago, Yamaha managed to create an intuitive sound generator that thrived on creativity. The most recent upgrades improve on the A3000's features, and with the A5000 offering huge amounts of effects, 124-note polyphony and loads of filters, it's the effects junkie's sampler of choice. Its major drawback, however, is its operating system, which at times could be the last strand of the Sumerian Bible. For a first-time buyer, this won't be a problem, but producers accustomed to another particular make will find themselves trying desperately to rename a sample bank.

EMU

Makers of the classic SP1200, EMU cater for every range of sample buyer. From high-end to entry-level models, EMU samplers are known for their sound-manipulation capabilities and built-in beat-mangling processors. Probably Akai's biggest threat in terms of market dominance, EMU samplers combine ease of use with creative capabilities. The major argument for EMU models lies in their compatibility with other formats and huge sound-manipulation potential.

Roland

Roland offers a number of studio options and has recently been the toast of NAMM (the International Music Products Association) and the music-technology world with its release of the VP9000, which allows you to modify pitch and tempo in real time literally at the touch of a knob. On the downside, you can buy a reliable second-hand car for less, and it only offers six-part polyphony. In all, it's certainly an indication of the trends that future samplers may follow, although not those within bedroom budgets.

soft samplers

As with the vast majority of hardware, programmers are constantly developing software alternatives. These are available from around £200 to upwards of £1,000. Many audio cards incorporate a sampler as part of their set-up. The major drawback of soft samplers is their tendency to hog huge amounts of processor memory, and they rarely offer the same amount of effects or sound-mangling ability. It's also unlikely that you'll want to lug your entire computer to a gig. On the plus side, however, they can be cheaper than outboard samplers, they have quicker loading times and they suit the travelling musician down to the ground if he's running off a notebook. An iBook with an audio-card sampler and some plug-ins should be all you need to travel the globe, creating music as you go.

more stuff

Every remixer and musician has his own equipment preference. If you want to do cinematic, orchestra-style reworkings, where parts are replayed live, a microphone and preferably some instruments are also required. Although with a bit of work a sampler can recreate almost any synth, most producers have at least one free-standing sound module. Samplers also run into problems recreating draw-bar organs, so rich and lucky people have outboard Rhodes and B3s. With an almost alarming array of boxes available, your best motto when acquiring equipment is to try before you buy. Some outboard effects are very desirable, not only for hands-on control and real-time knob twiddling, but also VST applications do have a nasty habit of sucking CPU power. (The types of effects units available are covered in Chapter 10.)

So, in the end, the decision is yours. There are literally hundreds of permutations when it comes to a home studio set-up, so my advice is to read magazines, try the machinery, if possible, and definitely don't believe the hype. Walking into some computer hardware shops can be a nightmarish vision of testosterone-fuelled wannabe garage producers arguing the tech specs on the brand new 9876-522AA or some equally obscure numerical-based bullshit that they've read about in some trendy techie sound mag but failed to understand.

From personal experience, I find that it's best to support your local retailer, who, aside from being unlikely to be swamped with demands from talentless egos, will have the time to build up a relationship with you and will hopefully recognise your needs and won't be tempted to fob you off with the latest model that clearly doesn't suit your requirements. In addition to staying local, contacting the product's manufacturer is a good way of obtaining information, albeit biased. Most companies will happily send out envelopes stuffed with glossy flyers, so research thoroughly and buy wisely.

ACID, Mixman and looping heaven

Sequencers aren't the only tools you can use to remix. Recently, a lot of platforms have sprung up with the home-based dance-music producer in mind, catering for people who don't want to immerse themselves in techie sequencing. As this book is aimed at full remixing, I'll provide only a basic overview here of what's available. For a fuller picture, check out Appendix 1, where you can find out where to obtain all of the relevant software.

Mixman

Developed by Beatnik, Mixman is an entire range of software that, like Beatnik sample CDs, aims to cover every base of small-scale home production. Mixman StudioPro, the flagship package, is a virtual DJ software environment that allows users to create or remix their own music or the latest music from major-label recording artists by using D*Plates, Mixman's "Internet singles". The tools include Remixing Studio for real-time, performance-based remixing; FX Studio for manipulating component sounds; Editing Studio for precision composition; and Recording Studio for adding personalised sounds into each mix. Unique to the Mac version is the ability to control the Remixing Studio using any MIDI keyboard or input device. Also, users are now able to export their sound-sets using Beatnik's own Rich Music Format (RMF), which provides a real-time listening experience that doesn't require streaming. Mixman StudioPro 4.0 is the first-ever product that couples Mixman's music-authoring capabilities with Beatnik's RMF technology.

Mixman's StudioPro 4.0 also enables users to publish their own work via the Internet, by allowing them to upload their creations to their own personalised homepage on the Mixman site, called My Mixzone. My Mixzone is personalised specifically for each user, enabling him to post his creations and invite his friends to listen and remix their own versions of sound-sets online. In addition, My Mixzone has photo capabilities, interchangeable skins and a map indicating the user's country of origin.

ACID

Created by Sonic Foundry, ACID is a family of genre-specific loop-based production tools which let you create "the kind of music you love". The tools in the ACID-style family use loops (ie clips of sound that can be strung together to sound like continuous music) which are then "painted" into a track. Combine a few tracks of loops and you've created a song. It's easy – just pick some loops, paint them into a track and then play them back. ACID comes complete with a whole range of genre-prepared loops, from hip-hop to techno. Some would argue that both Mixman and ACID are nothing more than powerful toys that endanger musical creativity by catering for a minority of style-dictated genres. You decide.

EJay

There's a good chance that you've seen a flimsy and CD-driven series of magazines nestling amongst *Wax* and *Future Music* offering demos of EJay, another loop-based sequencing program. Again, EJay is similar in nature to ACID and Mixman, although considerably cheaper and, some would say, more flexible. The major drawback here is that only a PC version is available.

chapter 5

and so it begins...

"Fnord."
Justin Case (The New Yorker)

what you get

OK, so you've been commissioned, hopefully by a good band and for good money. A courier is being sent from a respected studio or a dark heroin-encrusted bed-sit. But just what is he carrying in his triple-signed package?

Most songs you receive will be provided on A-DAT, a digital multitrack system employed by studios and home studio producers alike. Occasionally, you'll receive the original tapes, but this is becoming less likely as the digital revolution (less Marxist more Marx brothers) takes over the recording industry. The advantage of A-DAT is that you receive the track in its entirety, unmixed and separated. This allows you to pick the hooks in their unprocessed states and at the levels that you require. Of course, you do need an A-DAT player so that you can extract the audio, but the procedure itself is simple. You can either record the parts directly onto your sequencer or you can use a sampler to extract the snippets you'll need. Most studios have all formats of recording available, and if you've been commissioned you can request the format that you're going to be needing.

native sequencer format

Data on this format will come on floppy, zip or CD-ROM, and you load it as you would one of your own saved songs. This format gives you the advantage of being able to load the song in its entirety and see it visually, and it also enables you to work directly with the song. However, the main problems arise with MIDI and the selection of instruments that were used to record the piece. MIDI, as you know, is like notation or, better still, a series of signals that your computer relays to MIDI-implemented devices. If the devices are configured differently, there may well be sound clashes. It is, however, unlikely that you'll be sent just a MIDI map, with no audio samples.

WAV and AIFF files

These files are what your sampler uses to encode recorded audio onto a hard disk or some other storage medium. WAV files are native to PC-formatted media, while AIFF (or Audio) is the format preferred on the Apple Mac. It's possible that you'll be sent a disk of the individual parts encoded in such a way. Treat AIFF files just as you would samples on a sample CD. A lot of audio sample CDs include this digital format anyway as part of the package, so you may well already be familiar with them. They are cross-platform files, and hundreds of encoders for converting them are available to buy or download free over the Internet.

The kindly courier should also bring you a copy of the original song, if not the final mix, and if so then at least a rough mix will be provided. You should use this as your starting point. Try your best not to lose it.

basic formats

Here are some definitions of the most common audio formats. When I'm commissioned to do a remix, I find it best to put in a request for the files that suit me best.

- DAT (Digital Audio Tape) – This is often more correctly referred to as R-DAT, because the tapes use rotating heads, as do video cassettes. (Recorders using stationary heads are referred to, unsurprisingly, as S-DATs.) DAT machines operate in the same way as regular tape recorders – ie by pressing Record and Play. The difference, however, is the quality. DATs are the favoured medium for shipping remixes.

- A-DAT – A multitrack version of the above. The cassettes are the same size as video cassettes and each tape contains a maximum of eight tracks.

- Two-inch tape – The staple medium of studios everywhere and the standard straight-to-tape recording format favoured by traditional bands.

- Quarter-inch tape – A format popular decades ago and still used at the mixdown stage in some studios.

- <u>MiniDisc</u> – A format that is slowly becoming an accepted medium for home studio producers, who favour the compression it employs.

- <u>MIDI files</u> – Literally, computer files of MIDI information readable by all sequencers (depending on the type of MIDI used).

- <u>AIFF</u> – Mac-centric digital audio file.

- <u>WAV</u> – PC-format digital audio file.

approach, approach, approach

OK, so where do you start? How does A become A+B? Well, there is no concrete method of going about a remix, and unless you've been commissioned to work in a specific musical style, the song is your very own grit which you must rub into a pearl. (Remember, imperfection sometimes adds value.) In order to provide some perspective, I've gathered some comments here made by some other artists about their own approaches.

"It would start with the original vocal and nothing else. If we were going to do something involving me playing live then I would try not to hear any of the chords from the original and I would try and get some kind of weird harmonic twist on what's going on with the melody."
   Portishead

In many ways, this is one of the freest ways to approach remixing, by allowing yourself to create a backing track from scratch. This is definitely a case of defining your own style.

Meanwhile, Steve Rodway, who has remixed Dubstar and Diana Ross, approached Pulp's 'Common People' in this way: "I only take things which spotlight the performance of the record, and with 'Common People', for me it was Jarvis' vocal and the song itself, which shone out." His almost Europop backing track catapulted Pulp's single into the charts. (The original, like that of Cornershop's 'Brimful Of Asha', was confined to the true fans.)

Renowned for his classical reworkings, William Orbit approaches songs on a project-by-project basis: "I usually draw the sounds off the multitrack tape into my system. Every remixer has their own system, and you can incorporate whatever you want into that. Most people have data collated on some sort of computer system, whether it be Cubase, C-Lab or some sort of Mac-based system. I still use Cubase on an Atari Mega 2, though I've now also got a couple of Macs. Everybody's got their preferred sound-sampling and sound-creating equipment. I've got an Akai S3200, and these days I load everything into that and run the whole mix through the stereo outputs and into a couple of valve compressors. I compress it heavily and use everything on board the S3200. It runs very well and maintains the phase coherence, improving the impact of the sound. I still use my old Trident 80B desk. I love it!"

The commercially successful Rapino Brothers see their job as "just a question of altering the arrangement. Our job is to take a track, and that is what we are paid for," usually by taking large chunks of the original and adding beats.

However, the practice of using large chunks of a song isn't confined to the commercial domain. Autechre use only samples from the original: "Our remixes are all from the original. It's made from the original. Usually, it's all samples of the original track." This, however, doesn't limit the potential for manipulating sounds, and vastly different atmospheres can be created via sampler-tweaking and the application of effects.

Richard D James of Aphex Twin takes an altogether more laid-back approach: "I admit that sometimes I don't put any work into remixing at all. Sometimes I just give them an old, completely different track and say, 'Yeah, there's your remix.'"

It seems, then, that there are no rules, although a common approach seems to be to find the original record's signature. All remixers start from a building block taken from the original, whether this is the vocal line, an instrumental hook or a single bass note.

finding a hook

A hook is basically a central melody, usually a chorus. Most remixers will look for the hook as a place to centre the song or keep the integrity of the original (*à la* the bass line to Roni Size's 'Brown Paper Bag', the piano on 'Tosca' and the drop on 'Binary Fineries'). The hook can be as small as a vocal snippet (assuming that you're not using the entire vocal track), and this is especially important in club remixes as, for the most part, vocals and a house beat do not equal Handel's *Messiah*. Rather, the norm is the *Messiah* heard from a passing car. Minimal vocals are employed to cater for minimal attention spans.

"In many remixes, vocals are often so over-simplified that they sometimes become nothing more than a repetitive phrase or riff. When a track is remixed, the remixer may change the whole backing track, restructure the vocals, alter the tempo and even change the key, resulting in the vocals becoming so divorced from the music that the two elements are no longer dependent on each other."
    Phil de Costa

However, some tracks *do* require the minimum use of a vocal line. This is especially true if you've been commissioned by a major record label to produce a commercially viable track. (I'm not saying that the general public are conformist, ignorant fools who fear change, but, as Coldcut once said, innovation isn't particularly lucrative.) Some songs have no vocal lines at all, which can be seen as being either incredibly liberating or more constricting. After all, a vocal line can be devoid of links to music, which means that the remixer has a free run at the piece. But a central riff can exist in many contexts, or even just used sparingly as a background reminder of the original.

retaining the song's originality

It's probably appropriate to ask whether the hallmark of the original material (ie what makes the song what it is) needs to be kept at all. Again, this is largely determined by the circumstances of the remix. A large commission from a major label will obviously mean that the remix will have to retain its original direction, whereas commissions received by smaller companies and your own work won't need to rely so much on the original material. However, it's important to consult the band during the remixing process. Where do they want their song to be taken? After all, it is their song. (This is assuming that you're not an already established remixer, as it wouldn't be too cynical to think that some remixes are created purely for the sake of the name attached to them, such as The Orb's remix of Mike Oldfield "for credibility", or any Moby-style tag.) Building good working relationships with bands is an important factor in becoming a successful remixer.

Exploit technology. You can email versions, comments and audio data to the band and even keep up a running commentary of your progress. Unless you've been given full artistic licence, there's not a band I know who don't appreciate being asked their opinion first. The whole concept of originality is a very flimsy idea, so be specific when you ask questions and don't be intimidated by record companies who behave like dictatorial despots.

money

The big, bad capitalist worms ate the music industry's rotting core quite some time ago. That's not to say that ethics don't exist, of course – Ninja Tune are a perfect example of a company that is artistically conscious and successful – but remixing is big business, and I'm sorry to say that a lot of the bad press and stigma attached to it is due to the large sums of money that change hands.

Record companies can cash in easily. Follow a successful song with an associated big-name remix and there's good odds that the label that releases it will earn big-time, and so the practice of remixing runs a very real risk of being forever associated with chasing fast bucks. When you create a remix, you can expect to be paid anywhere from a couple of quid to over half a million dollars. The price is usually set and is determined by the size of the artist, the fame of the remixer and the desperation/generosity of the label.

The corporate cow that was remixing in the mid '90s is thankfully starting to evolve. Jason Swinscoe's Cinematic Orchestra successfully opened people's minds, thanks to his employment of the technique of creating "live" versions of personally selected tracks. (Swinscoe turned down a Moby remix on principle, and you can imagine the sums involved there!) Kruder And Dorfmeister, who raised the perception of remixing with *The K&D Sessions*, will only remix tracks that they like. They rarely take commissions and prefer to choose tracks to remix.

As the mainstream begins to mimic dance culture with the use of samples, artists like Fatboy Slim and Moby, however unoriginal, have brought reworking to the masses. Knowledge of dance-music production has led to a greater acceptance of remixes. Slowly, money will become less of a motivation, recalling perhaps the days of Bach and King Frederick, a monarch who regarded reworking as an artistic compliment. Giving weight to this hope are the wealth of websites that currently offer amateur remixes. The Internet is littered with countless websites containing songs reworked by fans, while parody versions of pop tunes cluster in their thousands at MP3 sites. It's now easy to download an audio ripper, take apart your favourite record, remix it and upload it to the web. Conscientious bands offer samples of their own work for just this purpose, notably Sofa Surfers, Björk and, more recently, Garbage and even Britney Spears. Remix competitions are another phenomenon that the Internet has prompted, and these are run by most music-technology and -production magazines, enlisting established artists to provide tracks to be remixed. Coldcut have even run a remix competition for charity.

The Internet and related projects provide a flickering glimmer of light. If music and samples are available, there is a hope that attitudes towards ownership will evolve. The Internet has the potential to be a vast and beautiful canvas where anyone can contribute to songs, interacting directly with their favourite artist's music. As this underwrites money, remixing and songwriting may genuinely achieve a heart. An unpaid remix is made with love or malice, either one of which is a better motivation than money. Imagine, if you will, a sprawling community defining a new language of shared creativity, of audio-visual sample exchanging and public-domain songwriting. This is quite possibly limp-wristed idealism, but the seeds are there.

In terms of your own remixing career, however, I would say that it's always best to go for your own preference of song over money. It's better in the long run, I assure you. Don't haggle with the payers, either. Some will actually ask you what you charge, so remember that you make music. Despite what Robbie Coltrane might say, you're not a banker.

oh, inspiration...

One of hardest problems when making a remix is to have an idea about the final product. You may have been commissioned to work within a generic style, but you still have to envisage the overall structure. There are many ways of doing this. What follows are some ideas for you to try out. Remember, they're just ideas, and certainly not proven or even preferential. They're only guides for you to expand on.

visual arrangements

"From the onset, you can picture the remix you're going to do."
    Rob, Autechre

As we are human, we are naturally disposed to think in pictures. Psychologists have long thought that the method of communication between the conscious and unconscious mind is pictorial and explain dreams as being visual conversations. In fact, there is a strong possibility that all thought is in some way rooted in visualisation, which means that it's one of our most potent thinking tools. Most modern musicians have become accustomed to thinking in such a way, particularly as sequencers and computer music applications are based around the visual representation of music.

Just try sitting and really listening closely to a piece of music (psychoactives or no psychoactives). Take notice of the feelings that you get, the associations that your brain makes and the pictures that your mind conjures. Hopefully, you'll begin to notice similarities within genres of music – certain sounds have certain colours. This is especially true in dance music, to which textures and builds are so vital. All of this knowledge can be used to make visual representations or maps of songs, a sort of blueprint or working basis for your remix.

Song maps can look however you want them to. They can detail every nuance of every part or just be a straight line showing the overall structure. Results are usually best if you map out the song that you've been commissioned to remix and work from that as your basis, changing the map.

Here are a couple of basic visual representations. They can be as simple as a curved line or as complex as something by Picasso.

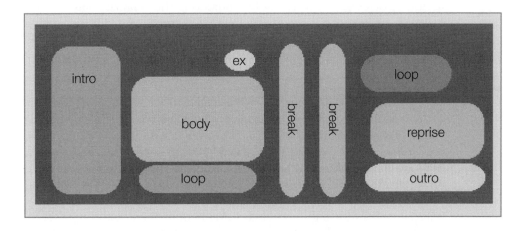

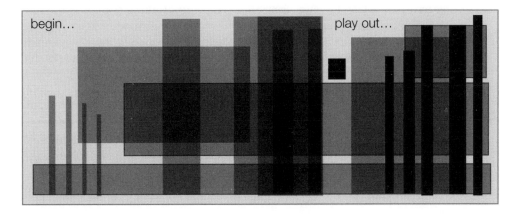

random is fun

Another technique you can use is simply to load a few samples into your sequencer and play around with them at random. Place them wherever your mouse will take them. Try reorganising an entire song from its composite samples. This approach will give results similar to Autechre's. Also, you could try putting different effects on different channels without worrying too much about what they'll do. Don't keep a sample set to a single channel. This might be a nightmare in mixdown, yes, but it's a good ideas generator. And remember serendipity, the happy accident. Exploit your mistakes.

maths?

Sure. Not maths rooted in the conventional sense of creativity, but you can apply mathematical formulae to samples and notes (no, seriously) and the order in which they appear will rely on changing the output number. For example, you start by numbering the original song samples 1, 2, 3, 4, etc, and then organise them into a pattern – 3, 2, 1, 4 – changing the pattern every time it repeats. Incidentally, I once heard that this is the technique employed by George Michael, so draw your own conclusions.

maths? not again…

I've also heard of topographical representations drawn onto sheets of music – ie an outline of the thing superimposed over a musical stave. Where there are obvious turns or angles, these could be taken as points to insert notes, or a long line would be a sustained note, etc. This sort of technique is a more technical extension of the visual approach outlined above. I've seen the "score" for a piece by John Cage which consists of a number of transparencies with lines and circles drawn onto them and a number of pages with constellations of dots on them. To perform the piece, you choose a transparency and a page, layer them, and the resulting graphic is the first page of the score, and so on. It's up to you to determine how to map the score to the music. This kind of technique can be applied if you've already done the remix but the record company and/or the band disapprove. In this case, simply replace the musical stave with the sequencer's screen.

sensible and simple

Of course, you can simply start off with your hook or vocal line and build your track around that. This is definitely the simplest and probably the most intuitive method of all. I tend to use this technique even when writing original material – doodling over a riff can produce very happy

AND SO IT BEGINS...

results. The other advantage of working with part of the original as a kick-off point is that it usually leads to a tighter-sounding remix, tailored as it is to the original.

mixing on the fly

Back before computer-based sequencers and even samplers of the most archaic nature, a remix was performed by "flying in" audio, literally remixing a track while importing audio in real time. This technique probably descended from the common Jamaican practice of reconfiguring or versioning a rhythm track into any number of new songs. By improvising and mutating its own repetitions of pre-recorded material, dub added something distinctly uncanny into the mix. This gave reggae and dub their trademark "spectres" and audio-warping. Although a very hit-and-miss and hugely time-consuming process, it's still worth having a go at mixing the original song in real time in this way, if you can. Try dropping parts out and adding effects, but keep the original structure. You probably won't be able to arrive at a final version in this way, but you'll certainly get a better feel for the track that you're working on.

blind mixing

This bypasses everything I've already said about getting to know the track that you're remixing. With this technique, you load only the samples you've received and try your best never to hear the original song, instead forming a song based on individual samples, rather than the concentric whole. This technique can be likened to working with found samples or sample CDs – no picture and no overall structure, just a series of yet-to-be-used building blocks. For variety, try loading some (but not all) of the original samples and then try using a different amount, working your way up to using all of the samples. Of course, you might run the risk of recreating the original track in this way, but a blow of synchronicity that large would kill a cow. (Personally, I don't find this method of great use, but it can be fun and it helps in achieving a degree of spontaneity.)

why bother?

As Richard D James of Aphex Twin pointed out earlier, you can always give the artist or commissioner a track that you've had lying around. (Of course, it's much easier to get away with this approach if you're in Aphex Twin!) A commercially viable trance reworking may raise a few eyebrows if your remix is a backwards sample of monkeys rutting without even the bass line hidden in the mix. People are unimaginative at the best of times – record companies

41

wouldn't exist without frontal lobotomies – so, if you feel you can't risk it, don't. It's better that the lowest common denominator has a second-rate remix to ram their heads against the wall to than some angry, confused label banging *your* head against a wall.

why does everything sound backwards?

One simple method is to work in reverse, creating an original track and slotting in the original samples later, although obviously it can be a tear-shedding event when your masterpiece doesn't even accommodate a single piano riff from the original.

cinematics

Another idea is to listen to a song, divide up its central parts and then play it again live. Having a band at your disposal helps here, but the versatility of MIDI should allow convincing results. Replaying bit parts is sometimes the only way to fit a riff into a remix with extreme changes in tempo. Often, live instruments also add immediate depth and a much-needed organic injection into dance music.

the avant-garde approach to creative blocks

If my memory serves, Brian Eno developed something called *oblique strategies*, a series of instructions listed on three-inch by five-inch cards, which assisted him when he hit an impasse while recording. The instructions were phrases such as "Accent something understated" or "Leave it going longer", which called his attention to what he was working with. You can draw up your own variation on this approach, although it may feel overly clinical.

Again, don't feel compelled to use any of these techniques. They should simply act as a guide and, hopefully, a springboard into the many approaches that are variously employed. Before you dive straight in, though, look at whatever initial idea you might have, no matter how seemingly small or insignificant, and keep referring back to it at every impasse. The answers are there, so just keep looking and rethinking your ideas in any way you can.

serendipities

Literally meaning "happy accident", serendipity is at the heart of creation. All artistic endeavours, however well thought out, are met in some way or another by mistake – accidents will happen, as the saying goes. However, mistakes are certainly not always the realm of despair and desperate reworking. Just like Colombus' accidental discovery of the Americas, mistakes in music sometimes turn average songs into works of genius.

One of the classic tales of serendipity concerns Motown's legendary sound. Very possibly a myth created by lacklustre producers who've supped once too often at the font of mediocrity, the tale concerns the record company's desk. Like all record companies, Motown started off in a cheap studio and small premises. After producing some of the greatest pop music ever to reach the public, they naturally upgraded, overhauling their entire studio. However, something was amiss. As soon as they started recording on the new premises, their sound changed. No longer were they producing with that hallmark warmth associated with their previous productions. After much detective work, they finally traced the discrepancy to the desk. Their new model worked fine, but it turned out that the original desk had a fault, and it was this error that helped to produce some of the most admired music ever created. Error sometimes works in your favour, so mistakes aren't always your enemy – although, of course, glaring errors are.

But how can you best work with the pieces you have in order to bring about such diversions? Firstly, as a producer, it's your job to recognise what's good and what's blatantly wrong, although of course there's a grey area between these extremes, and some would argue that it's this tightrope that great musicians consistently walk. Never approach a remix – or, for that matter, a song – with closed ears. If you screw up playing a piece, don't delete it immediately. Listen to how it sounds. If your cursor slips, play the arrangement anyway.

Some more superstitious artists believe that there's an inherent life to musical pieces. If a song or riff is supposed to sound a certain way then chaos and mistakes will dictate its final outcome. Simply be more attuned to what you're doing and try to be sensitive to musical possibilities.

Jason Swinscoe and Cinematic Orchestra

"Art is the perpetual motion of illusion. The highest purpose of art is to inspire. What else can you do? What else can you do for anyone but inspire them?"
  Bob Dylan

"I'll play it first and tell you what it is later."
  Miles Davis

Throughout the writing of this book I've been struck again and again by the honest and friendly nature of the people who have helped me out. I thought that many of the featured artists in this book would be almost unapproachable at the outset, yet they all proved to be down-to-earth people with a genuine passion for what they do.

Jason Swinscoe is just such a person. The man behind Cinematic Orchestra and J Swinscoe Presents holds a special place in the realm of remixing. His remixes are the Pynchon of the dance world – often admired, seldom duplicated and occasionally misunderstood. Working firmly under the banner of integrity, Jason has transformed songs into things of originality. Straying away from the flock-driven cash chase, he chooses to work with "selective" material, deconstructing songs to their bones to find the original riff or inspiration. He then builds his remixes from the same starting point as the original artist, enlisting the help of his live band. His method of working creates remixes that are as valued as the originals on which they are based, songs that have the ability to exist in their own right rather than simply house tunes that nod at the original vocal lines. Cinematic Orchestra's impressive *Remixes* album is available as a stand-alone work. This is a testament to the quality of Swinscoe's work, here deemed good enough to constitute an album consisting of purely remix work.

I disturbed Jason on a sleepy Thursday morning to ask about his approach and began by establishing some background. Jason, who is Scottish, spent his childhood roaming from place to place, as his parents had itchy feet. To prove it, they spent their time moving around Yorkshire, and while enduring the constant trial of fitting in, changing horizons and coping with a rich Scottish accent down south, Jason somehow discovered music.

His first hands-on experience of music was with a guitar, but he only ever had a few lessons (another by-product of the constant moving). Despite this, he experimented by playing along with records and just jamming. In a way, music became his constant companion in an otherwise restless life. Then, after the rigmarole of school, he opted for a degree in Fine Art. It was at university that he formed a hardcore outfit, a three-piece with Jason playing bass. Slowly music began to be his favoured pursuit, with art a close second. In his own words, "Unfortunately, my degree suffered for my music."

After university, Jason returned home to do what everybody has to do, post-education, and got his life together. Music was clearly an inviting avenue...

The Evolution Of Style

TP: "How did you get from hardcore to jazz?"

JS: "After university, I went back to my parents and started listening to a lot of jazz-based music. That's where I discovered Ninja Tune and Mo'Wax. I started getting into DJing and turntables. I found that really interesting, in that you can combine two records to create a new record rather than just mixing in a record to the end of another record. I played the records simultaneously, just let the records play and [kept] them in time. You could start the records at different points and occasionally two different hooks would just match or harmonise. Certain bars would just sync, which triggers off different ideas. I think turntables can be a lot more interesting than just mixing house – which I did do, at a point, to get used to the decks. Get technique, you know?

"The next step was when I got into recording. I started taking little loops from records and realised quite quickly that all this music was heavily loop based, rooted around bars of 4/4 layered together, so I got a computer and sampler. At that point, I started going back to my old jazz records and realising it actually would be easier writing something in 4/4 instead of sampling. I found it really difficult. Each rhythm in jazz seemed to be different. I found I couldn't find a bass part for that drum part or a drum part for that lead part, so I thought I'd write the part.

"Basically, I found it quite restrictive. Computers and samplers are great, but when you start working outside of 4/4 it starts to get difficult. I'm actually really interested in time signatures – say, taking a 6/4 and slowly, over however many bars it takes, resolving it into a 3/12. There's this guy called Steve Coleman who does incredible stuff and he does it live. He's really into...well, equations, I guess. The drummer will be playing 9/4, the bassist in a different signature and eventually they modulate together. These kinds of people kind of push it a bit."

Cinematic Orchestra eventually came about in 1997 after Jason recorded five tracks at Blow Yard Studios, after which the group – "a collective of musicians and film-makers" – came slowly into being. The line-up, although organic, reads as follows: Tom Chant on soprano saxophone, Phil France on acoustic/electric bass, T Daniel Howard on drums, Alex James on piano, Jamie Coleman on trumpet/flugelhorn and Patrick Carpenter on turntables/electronics. Eva Katzenamaier co-produced some of the tracks with Swinscoe, but the bulk of her Cinematic Orchestra work is done with Ben Drew, as a film-maker. She also collaborated on the remix album. While there are quite a number of other people involved, some contribute on a looser basis than others.

TP: "Could you talk us through the *Remixes* album?"

JS: "The *Remixes* album was from the first album, *Motion*, which came out in 1999 [and] was a combination of technologies and live instruments."

TP: "Do you use sampled drums or do you program? Because the drums are quite complex to the average programmer."

JS: "A combination of both, really. On the live recording, there will be a drummer, sax, piano, bass. It will all be played in the room. I'll take the piano melody and the rhythm and send it through to the control room, who'll loop it up and play it back out into the session room and we'll mess around and come up with ideas and jam for ten minutes or so and see what comes out."

TP: "Like a jazz session?"

JS: "It's based around structure. We'll leave the rhythm part in and take the melody part out and jam around with that – there's a lot of freedom in the piece. Then we'll take all the live material and stick it into the computer [and] maybe cut it up. Cut up some drums. The aim is to keep the music sounding live. It can be quite tricky, but at the end of the day, when you listen to the track on the album and you can't hear any joins, it's a good feeling. It can excite a lot of people."

TP: "What software do you use?"

JS: "Cubase, my computer, an old Mackie desk [and] piano. It's [about] trying to keep the feel, in the end, so you can feel the individual playing, trying to add the subtleties and accents while programming and ending up with a piece of music that you want."

TP: "How do you translate that live? Do you DJ over a band?"

JS: "I don't DJ. I play the keyboard to trigger off samples from part of the song, whether it's a melody line or...a number of different things. The other guys are bass, drums, sax. The trio's background was jazz. Everybody from the band has come from a different aspect of jazz or dance. I've been through a few drummers. I don't know why. I think they explode at every gig! I've got a new drummer now called T Daniel

Howard, Phil France plays bass and piano, Tom Chant is sax and brass. T Daniel Howard is a brilliant drummer. He can actually recreate all the little intricate bits from the programming. It's part of the charm to be able to recreate that live so there's a good foundation on which to start. So there's quite a bit of room to experiment. The live show is quite a different experience."

TP: "Are you touring at the moment?"

JS: "At the moment we're concentrating on the new album."

TP: "What's the new material like? Is it in a similar vein?"

JS: "It's different. I sent a couple of tracks to Ninja and they were surprised at how different it was. It was my intention to keep it different."

TP: "There was quite a dark edge to the first album."

JS: "Yeah, it was quite moody. On the new album, some of the tracks are lighter to the touch. It's more in the fact that's it's more up-tempo than down…"

TP: "Like the track you did with Patrick Carpenter, 'Neptune' [a track on the *Xen Cuts* compilation with PC, one of the many sides of DJ Food]."

JS: "Yeah, exactly. We decided not to use either of our names, Cinematic Orchestra or DJ Food, but decided on a different one altogether. I didn't want the new album to sound exactly the same as *Motion*."

TP: "Did you approach the *Remixes* album the same as you approached *Motion*?"

JS: "Yeah. I'll get a part from the original, say, on DAT, then stick it on the computer and then go into the studio for a session, the same way as on the first album. Generally, my thoughts on remixing [are] that it's a remix, but in a way I want to give a little bit extra, rather than just to take it all apart and just re-edit. I'm taking it right down, right down, then taking it back up. Because the original versions are one riff, so are these. It's like a whole new song."

TP: "That's the way classical musicians used to rework their stuff."

JS: "Yeah. And in a way, that's where the ideas have come from. It's taking that fundamental idea and saying, 'We'll take that and do that,' and reworking it."

TP: "In terms of originality, remixing has come under a lot of criticism – money-spinning and so on. Where do you think originality ends and remixing begins?"

JS: "Basically…being able to deliver a track that you can say, 'Here's the original,' and going, 'Oh yeah, that's that sound,' but being a different listen, as it were. A new sound. Maybe using the same sound or vocal line. I think that's how remixes should be. It's also that maybe the marketing department may use the same piece of music but for different markets. It's quite greedy. It doesn't necessarily mean that's its new music."

TP: "You famously turned down a Moby remix."

JS: "Yeah I think a lot of people would have jumped at it. I have to admit that my initial reaction was, well…a Moby remix? I said yeah before I actually heard it. But after I calmed down, I reconsidered. In a way, I've got big respect for what he's done and doing. I don't mean any disrespect. It just doesn't do anything for me. You can say at the moment his tunes are very catchy and immediate. My girlfriend would have slapped me. I said, 'What would you say if one side of a twelve-inch was me and the other was Paul Oakenfold?' I felt really good about not doing it. People were saying, 'Well, you could have sold thousands of copies,' but in the end I'm not really that bothered."

TP: "There is quite a wide selection of music on the *Remixes* album."

JS: "Yeah. I had people on the *Remixes* album that were relatively well known, like DJ Krust, Piero Umiliani and Faze Action – they go on and on but, you know, I met them not long ago and they were really nice guys."

TP: "Did they come to you with the remixes or did you approach them?"

JS: "They came to me. There's only seven songs. One of them is a remix of a cinematic track."

TP: "That's 'Channel One Suite'."

JS: "That's right. It never really came out. I had bigger ideas. This is probably the first and last time I give someone a remix. Hefner did a remix that was just an edit, really. I respect people who have a true spirit for music, and Hefner does, but I wanted more, really. It kinda made me want to do remixes for other people and spend time on [them], not churn [them] out. I've consciously stopped remixing at the moment. It actually takes up a lot of time. I tend to spend about three weeks on one remix, which I guess is quite a long time. I remember, when I was doing the remixes, taking them into Ninja, they would ask, 'Is this a new track?' And I'd be, 'No, it's another remix.' They kept asking me why I was giving away all these great pieces of music. I was doing remixes because either I liked the original piece of music or I actually liked the person and his ideas. I was really excited to start with. Maybe again in the future. A lot of the people who have asked, I would really like to do them, but not at the moment."

TP: "You're at home experimenting with styles?"

JS: "It can be quite an interesting idea if the producers try new styles, but if the tune or dance doesn't have any character then it's not really worth it and often a let-down [from] a normally good artist."

TP: "What do you think of what's going on in the charts? It seems like riffs just keep being regurgitated over and over with a new beat."

JS: "I do listen to the charts now and again but I don't really follow it. But it does tend to be a nice guitar riff in a song, but then, in a month, it will be in a different song and you're left thinking, 'What? I just listened to that!' It's all manufactured in the charts, anyway, so there's a definite generic chain. There's a program on at the moment called *PopStars*."

TP: "Yeah. Compulsive for all the wrong reasons."

JS: "It's just hilarious. There was this bloke on the other night who said, 'I don't want to go home and look in the mirror and just be nobody.' I mean, it's hilarious. It worries me, actually, that these people are more and more worried that they will be nobody, and that these things are right. Everyone goes on about the cult of celebrity. Pop is all about celebrities; it's not about music."

TP: "But there's still the underground, which is still going strong. People get paid a lot more for producing pop. But then, I guess there's always been a lot of pop about, if you look at the '50s or '60s."

JS: "Yeah, but it was a different kind of music back then. In the '60s, it had a bit more of an honest feel to it. It's become more manufactured and tailored now. But getting back to remixing, my main aim with the tracks I did was to show them a bit of respect and try to do my best, which sometimes meant the remix sounded like a different piece of music. And because I was generally remixing artists who I liked, they respected the difference. They didn't turn around and say, 'Well, that's not what I wanted.'"

TP: "So you had full artistic say on the remixes?"

JS: "Um…well, the people who approached me just came to me and said, 'We want a remix.' I'm doing a track for Hefner at the moment – sort of returning the favour – and he said he wanted me to keep the vocal. It's a vocal-driven track. But later he came back to me and said, 'Just do what you want.'"

TP: "What advice would you give to someone approaching a remix?"

JS: "Treat it as your own music. Don't do it for money. If you're thinking about developing your own career then you're only as good as your last piece of music. In a way, that's kind of harsh, but true. Concentrate everything into it, all your knowledge up to that point, and don't be afraid of wasting your interesting ideas. Only accept a remix if you want to do it. If you're not doing it 100 per cent, you'll wind up ballsing it up or making a mediocre job of it. That's why I'm not concentrating on remixing for a bit, 'cause my heart's not in it, and your heart has to be in everything you do."

TP: "Could you tell us a bit about The Loop?"

JS: "The Loop is basically a collective of people – Ben, who does the visuals for our live show; our sax player; myself; and a few other people. Basically, a couple of years ago, we wanted to set up a club and we thought we'd collaborate and do a club together.

"Our music policy was pretty loose, from free jazz, soul and funk to whatever, all rolled into one. Ben, being the visual guy, was, like, 'Yeah, well, we want visuals,' so we looked at the clubs that were around and the sort of projection stuff that was going on, and it was just wallpaper, really. It might be nice to look at, but it didn't relate to the music. So we thought, 'How [can] we get a proper link?'

"I'd always wanted to set up a club that was to do with film, and we thought about what had been done in the past with film. We decided on DJing over films, but that's not that great. Instead of just playing music over a film, we thought it'd be good to have extra channels on the mixer so the audio from the film became an actual track. DJs then almost have the job of scoring the film – they can bring up pieces of dialogue or chunks of soundtrack and retell the story. We managed to separate the dialogue and the soundtrack using VHS."

TP: "What films did you use?"

JS: "The films being played were generally contemporary, and we asked producers and DJs who wanted to play to pick their own films. It worked really well. It gave people opportunities to explore the films a bit more and experiment with different tensions and release. Sparse films could become heavily orchestrated, and it would change the whole impetus of the film. One guy actually bpm'd all the dialogue and put breakbeats behind it so they were in time, which was really clever – you had people dancing as they watched a film. The other nice side-effect was the wide variety of music played, because people could swing into dialogue and back into music. DJs didn't have to play beat-matched stuff."

TP: "You've recently taken the cinematic theme a step further…"

JS: "Yes. Last year we were asked to go to Portugal and do a soundtrack for a movie. It was a really wonderful experience. They asked us to do an original soundtrack for *The Man With A Camera*, and it's an amazing film, a really beautiful film. Basically, the film's about this guy with a camera just going around filming different scenes. Just ordinary people doing ordinary things. There is no real story line, but the film is kind of broken up into a day. So, in the morning, you have a woman waking up with birds outside and people walking. Then it would cut to a factory with men working. It had a lot of very rhythmic scenes and it would slow down and trace the day through work, lunch, recreation, bars, etc. There's a section halfway through the film with a baby being born, people at a registrar's office…people in churches, at funerals… So it's almost like trying to put a score to life. There's actually a couple of tracks on the new album that are from the film."

TP: "How did you score it?"

JS: "Well, it was a project that all of [the band] were involved in…so we spent a week in the studio with all our instruments and a little TV and video. Actually, we even brought some other things, anything that would make sound. We would all swap instruments and just play around, hitting metal objects and stuff.

"Once it was done, we all went to Portugal and performed it live in front of 3,000 people, which was pretty scary, [but] it went down really well. We're going back next year, and hopefully we'll bring it to England."

One of the most inspiring things about Cinematic Orchestra is their hunger to take the medium further, rescoring films and recreating the concept of playing live. One could pretentiously venture that the project in Portugal was the ultimate expression of remixing, taking a film and imagining that the arguments for the existence of an *auteur* are true, in which case a film's meaning is as readily conveyed in its soundtrack as in its iconography. Changing a score and performing it live could be one of the few valid methods of remixing cinema. As Jason said, at The Loop, people chose to accentuate tensions that were ignored in the original film. Music enables a personal reading of somebody else's work. Barthes would chuckle at the concept, I'm sure.

If you approached the work with the consideration and sensitivity to the original that Cinematic Orchestra employed, you could easily end up with a rewarding concept of remixing, not just rehashing someone else's ideas but adding your own experience to someone else's vision. (The ideas of visual remixing, or audio-visual manipulation, are explored in Chapter 12.)

and the music?

Samples exist happily alongside live versions of themselves. The method that Cinematic Orchestra have developed points to one way out of the sample cul de sac; but, as Jason has stated before, not everything he hoped for is achievable yet: "I think the main thing is to make the most of the technology, whether you can get exactly what you want or not."

Richard Dorfmeister and the chronicles of dub

I visited Vienna for the first time at the end of 2000 and was struck by the nature of the city. In Vienna, coffee-houses that I thought were a fictional device used by Parisian intellectuals really do exist. In fact, not only do they exist but they co-exist with some of the most inventive production and sounds modern music has to offer. The Vienna sound has long been cited as being one of the true driving forces of trip-hop (for want of a better word) and dub.

Richard Dorfmeister and Peter Kruder have been responsible for creating a great deal of what we now call the Vienna sound. Their remix album *The K&D Sessions* is synonymous with not only quality remixing but also quality music. What follows is a brief interview with Richard Dorfmeister, who you'd be forgiven for thinking only works under the K&D guise. In actual fact, he is probably one of the most hardworking men in music, juggling running his record label, G-Stone, with writing and producing under Tosca, Stereotyp and Dr Richard – all this while DJing, remixing and, of course, working with

Peter Kruder. Part of K&D's charm is their ability to flirt with the mainstream (they have remixed Madonna and their tunes sit gracefully on various red-eye, comedown compilations) but never to lose musical integrity or their beliefs in what they are doing.

TP: "Firstly can you tell us a bit about your background, from Sin to your involvement with Peter?"

RD: "Well, that's quite a long story. I met Andi Orel when I was spinning records here in Vienna and he is still one of the best graphic artists around. I have a lot of respect for his works over the past years. He is one of the originals in this city. We started Sin together with him and Mona Moore. We did simple songs and translated them into electronic dimensions. Then I did a track with Rodney Hunter – that must have been 1990 – then a track with Patrick Pulsinger called 'City Lights'… This was the early Vienna period, when everybody was still experimenting with styles and concepts. It was a wild and moving time. But when I started working with Peter, in 1992, the whole thing started to get into shape. We both had tracks running and we jammed together, which led into the release of the *G-Stoned* EP. That was released in 1993 and started a chain-reaction which is still active…"

TP: "What are your beliefs, in terms of music – integrity, influence, etc?"

RD: "Quality rules. Everything goes. Music is the spice of life. Life is empty without love and music. Music keeps you going. Dub is the answer."

TP: "Tell us about the Austrian music scene."

RD: "Initially non-existent, now in full blossom. You find a lot of good labels and music people coming from diverse musical corners. There are some key movers here, and fresh releases are coming in all the time. Labels adjacent to our sound are Uptight, Klein, Couch, Vienna Scientists, Sunshine, Dubclub, etc. There is certain sound that is a mixture of deep grooves that has its roots in the love of black and dub music, which have a long history here already. The club scene is vivid but on the underground side, still friendly and not commercialised like in bigger cities like London or Paris. On Monday at the Flex there is a family vibe going on that is deep and full of heart… On more cynical views of the Viennese backgrounds, I can advise to read Werner Geier's article to be found in *The G-Stone Book*, released by G-Stone Recordings."

TP: "Has the nature of Vienna influenced the Vienna sound?"

RD: "It's strange here. On the one side, it is so beautiful here. On the other side, everybody has to escape from time to time… But especially the winter time here is relatively long, so the people in Vienna don't get so much sun. Of course, London is much rougher, weather-wise, but the weather always has an impact on the music-making process.

"The coffee-houses are fantastic. You will only find this variety here in Vienna. If you dig deep here you may find hidden treasures, but you have to stay positive, because Vienna sometimes drags you down. But then again, in 15 minutes you are in the countryside, which is simply wonderful."

TP: "You've expressed your alliance with low frequencies in a few articles I've read. When I talked to Matt Black, he brought up the idea of frequencies influencing biology and thought. He even went as far as to say that music, combined with visual stimuli, could act as a medium for remixing consciousness. Apart from influencing mood, do you think this is possible?"

RD: "Definitely. All sorts of frequencies are penetrating us all the time, with greater positive or negative impact… My theory is, if you are surrounded by good music, you are safe, protected by the magical frequencies of feeling good… When we are doing our live shows with Fritz Fitzke, I feel the power that music and visuals can have on your moods… I love to turn people on. When you connect with the crowd and your music, that's simply fantastic… Somehow, deep frequencies are touching our souls heavily, and that affects our hearts."

TP: "Is there a relationship between sound and colour? Can it be mapped, like a scale?"

RD: "Colours are essential. I love the concept of colours and the effect they can have on you, but at the end of the day you have to invent different kinds of stimulation to keep the inspiration alive. Personally, I tend to [prefer] darker colours. I am not so much into bright, shining colours when it comes to our cover designs. These low colours seem to have a longer life and reflect more our state of mind."

TP: "Can you tell us about Tosca and illuminate readers as to who Rupert Huber is? What can we expect from Tosca?"

RD: "Tosca is my old schoolfriend Rupert and me. We [have been] doing tracks for the last six years. Rupert is an excellent musician who is based in the more experimental art environment. At the moment, we are working on new tracks for the next album, due out in 2002. We are working hard to achieve something that impresses ourselves, since the level in terms of ideas is high, but in the end we just love to do new music and release it. It's still pure magic to infect the world with new sounds."

TP: "Will there be more Kruder And Dorfmeister releases, or are you concentrating on your solo projects?"

RD: "I love to see a new K&D release, and there will be something, but we'll wait for the right moment. It has to blow you away… All the original K&D works have been more than just another release – they have to be a killer. I think we only want to release killer tracks this year. The first release will be the new Stereotyp meets Tikiman. The track is called 'Jahman', and this track is definitely serious!

"I think it's good not to release too much under our names. We don't need to over-expose ourselves, and we are still in full control of our activities, fully independent."

TP: "*The K&D Sessions* album is synonymous with remixing. Can you tell us how that came about?"

RD: "*The K&D Sessions* was the result of four years' work on remixing. [Actually], it wasn't so much remixing; it was more like inventing new tracks, using little bits of other stuff while keeping the initial idea alive. At first, we wanted to release the sessions ourselves, but it was hard to get the rights from the majors, so we worked together with Studio !K7 in Berlin and they did a very good job. We worked pretty tight with them. The communication was good. Everything worked out."

TP: "How do you and Peter work together?"

RD: "At the moment, we're releasing the Stereotyp twelve-inch together. This will be a killer release. Stereotyp has developed his [own] style, [which] features fresh-sounding electronics with a modern dub and ragga style… After our Madonna release, we got away from the remixing and more into producing full-length albums with a special idea. That has been more fun and more motivating for us recently. There are a lot of things scheduled this year, also. It's gonna be slamming!"

TP: "Did you pick the artists on *Suzuki In Dub*?"

RD: "Yes. I wasn't really looking for people; I was just taking people on board who were around. Everything fell into place quite naturally. It's always an adventure, when you hand over your tracks to somebody and you're hoping that this guy has enough passion and time to do something on the track that isn't there yet. But all in all I was lucky to pick the right ones. Most of the mixes in the Tosca series were fine and successful. *Suzuki In Dub* had a nice cover idea, done by Sarah Littasy. She did the *Suzuki* album design as well, and this whole sort of family kind of production is something I love. The closer you are to every step in the production [process], the better is the result!"

TP: "What set-up are you using?"

RD: "Quite simple – computer, sampler, mixer [and] keyboards sort of set-up. We more and more love to play and sample ourselves – that is good fun and challenging – but at the end of the day it's more about good ideas than all this gear. You can go to a proper studio with a big mixing desk to get a proper sound, but I prefer lo-fi productions with ideas more than no ideas with high-end sound."

TP: "How do you usually approach a remix?"

RD: "As I said, we normally do a new track, twist it around completely, pump new blood into the original… That can be a pain, sometimes, if you lose yourself in a wrong corner, but if you get a good groove going and everything is flowing then it's easier. You act like [you're] in [a] trance. [It's] a great feeling to do a track and you know it is working out."

TP: "Can a remix be just a personal comment on another's song?"

RD: "For us it is a highly personal thing, since we invest two to three weeks in such a track. But, as I said, we are more into investing two to three weeks into our tracks now. That makes more sense, anyway."

TP: "How did you transform 'Transfatty Acid' by Lamb? I've listened to the original numerous times but still can't understand how you transformed it into such a masterpiece. Be as technical as you like!"

RD: "Just did it without thinking too much…"

TP: "Where do you find inspiration?"

RD: "Sweet inspiration is like a bird – it's hard to catch, and suddenly it's gone… I think I find inspiration in other people's music and in meeting and talking to different kinds of [people]. Honestly, I don't know. But suddenly it is here, and then I try to translate it into something useful."

TP: "You program most of the drums. What software/sequencer do you use? And is there a secret behind that vast warm Vienna sound?"

RD: "No secret, just a feeling that people try to achieve. It's about catching this very moment, like achieving a special sort of truth. What is interesting about the Vienna sound is the fact that the musicians get better and better with the productions now. Recently I am more and more impressed [by] what comes out of this city...

"Software-wise, we use Cubase...because we were [using] Cubase on the Atari for such a long time and the program has become sort of an old friend. You can't just get rid of these things like that... Anyway, nowadays you can do everything on your laptop with integrated software samplers, plug-ins and stuff. This is great, since you can do music anywhere you go, and not necessarily in your studio. That can be fresh and inspiring. Sometimes it's good to check out other studios to get a new view on things."

TP: "Do groups like Toxic Lounge, The Sofa Surfers and yourself all meet, or is the overall sound coincidence?"

RD: "More coincidence, but we see each other from time to time."

TP: "How do remixes – your own and others – influence DJing?"

RD: "I think DJing influences the production a lot. This drive you get on the road is essential for the studio work. All the reactions on records let you get a intensive feeling. Sometimes it is better to make a break and forget about dancefloors. Then it is just about pure music and nothing about bpms."

TP: "It could be said that the sets you play are actually real-time remixes of the records. Would you agree that mixing, in a sense, is a type of reworking?"

RD: "Sort of, but the work in the studio is much harder if you want to get something good. DJing is more about understanding situations, being on time, playing the right stuff at the right moment. But if you have the right set-up and you are able to have a sampler and some effects units with your records, you can do much more than simply play records. But, as with everything, the more often you do it, the better you get."

TP: "What, in your opinion, is a good remix?"

RD: "There are too many good remixes to mention, but if the basic material is a classic then it's hard to do something equally good. It's much easier to improve a track that's lacking something."

TP: "How do you view the current club scene?"

RD: "Very positive. In Vienna, there are a number of good clubs, and especially the Flex has the best sound system ever. Really, I have been travelling a lot over the past years and the Flex rules the area!"

TP: "Tell us about G-Stone, Ethos, practice artists, etc."

RD: "Our philosophy is somehow anti and hard to understand, definitely not the usual business sort of attitude – more relaxed, but with a strong focus on taste and quality. Perhaps things take longer at G-Stone, but the results are normally satisfying."

TP: "What advice would you give prospective musicians doing remixes?"

RD: "Treat a remix as if it is your own song."

TP: "Any closing comments, ideas or things you think people should know?"

RD: "Look out for forthcoming releases by Stereotyp, Tosca and K&D this year. And do something illegal."

chapter 6

cut it up

"So free and fluid but still like clockwork."
D Mavis on Mozart

what exactly can't you smell?

An invaluable tool in any respect, but especially in remixing, is the ability to cut and splice audio accurately. The visual representation in most sequencers is more than adequate for seriously mashing up sounds in the pursuit of arranging bass lines and generally shaping original tracks.

Assuming that you have a basic knowledge of how your sequencer operates, you should have no problem in following this exercise. Provided in the accompanying CD are a number of sound files, and you'll find the files relevant to cutting in the folder marked "Cut-Ups". (Logical, you see?) The first file you'll see here will be called "Smell". This is an audio file of a man

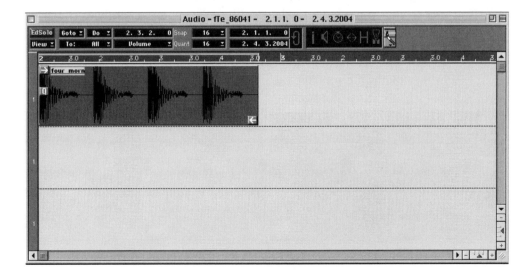

saying, "I don't smell it." "So?" I hear you cry. Well, the aim is to change "I don't smell it" into a different phrase. To begin with, import or drag the audio file onto your sequencer and then, once loaded, loop the sample. Then bring up the Wave Editor and set the quantise and snap values to 128 (or the maximum that your sequencer will allow), which will make for greater precision when splicing.

In the Wave Editor, you'll see four distinct waveforms:

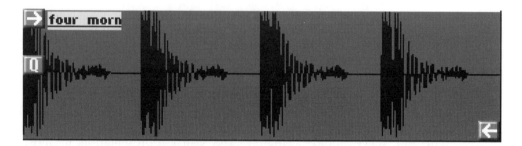

Each waveform is a word (ie "I", "dont", "smell" and "it"). Simply select the scissors or the appropriate cutting tool and slice the waveform into four separate pieces. Try to cut where the waveform is totally flat (ie approximately in the middles of the spaces).

Once you've done this, drag all of the parts out of the loop section into the "Appended Events" part of the window. You're now free to reorganise your samples at whim. (You may want to play each part with the Listen tool so that you know exactly which waveform corresponds to which of the four words.)

To start with, try making the man – let's call him Bob – say "I smell" simply by moving the appropriate parts into the appropriate order:

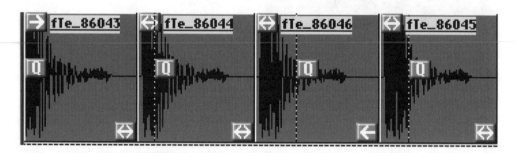

Then try making Bob say "I don't smell", then "it don't smell" and then "smell it". Just play around with different combinations. Try reversing just one waveform (this command will probably be in the Audio Functions menu of your sequencer), add effects and see how twisted you can make it. (For instance, time-stretch the whole thing to achieve sugar-daddy overtones.) Experiment – it might be worthwhile. If you're having difficulty, it's possible to view the waveform in terms of dynamic events, which will hopefully help you to narrow down where you want to slice.

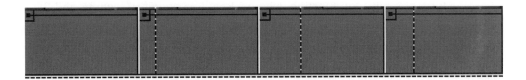

Another useful technique is to layer waveforms by copying them over each other. This is the sound of Fatboy Slim. You can create rises, builds and bouncing-ball effects by mimicking the above picture. The same applies to drums, snare rolls, floor-tom shudders and Aphex nastiness, all of which rely on the heavy use of cuts layered together.

Now look back in the "Cut-Up" folder, where there's a simple bass line and a breakbeat for you to experiment with. Just use the above instructions.

Rexx files and beat-mashing software

The job of cutting has been made a great deal easier in the last few years. With recent progress in sampling technology and programs like Steinberg's ReCycle, most of the hard work is done for you. If you load a sample into ReCycle, it will cut it up for you, finding the lowest wave points or zero crossovers. The sliced sample can then be exported as a Rexx file (ie a pre-sliced sample). This idea of sample slicing was probably first developed by early jungle producers who wanted to work with individual parts of a sample at different times. Some of the software that's available for beat-mashing is listed below.

ReCycle's Rexx files can be loaded directly onto a sampler and one sample mapped over a series of keys. The sample can then be triggered by a MIDI map (also produced by ReCycle) on your sequencer. The advantage of Rexx files is that they allow you to change the tempo of a piece without affecting its pitch or timbre, so to jack up a ballad to 180bpm without losing the vocal hook simply slice your vocals thinner than salami. Of course, most modern samplers will allow you to change tempo and pitch independently, but it usually takes more time and effort than just exporting a couple of files.

beat-mashing

A simple breakbeat is the staple diet of most producers, and there are literally thousands of sample CDs of them available. But, as you know, a simple breakbeat is just that: simple, clichéd and usually boring. Many samplers – most notably those produced by EMU and Yamaha – offer some form of remix loop function, where a loop is assigned to sections and then moved around at random. This occasionally produces some wonderful results, but on the whole these are serendipitous. Most sequencers allow a much more hands-on option, free from random chance, especially when used with a program like ReCycle.

Follow the process described above to load in a sample and open it in the Wave Editor window. Then cut the sample into its separate waves – unless you're using a Rexx file. (You may want to zoom in on the wave to slice close-clipping cymbals. Ideally you'll want your bass drum, snare and cymbals to be independent for maximum mobility.) Now loop and press Play on your sequencer, listening for clicks or any notable discrepancies in the loop. Clicks are caused when you cut audio away from a zero crossover point, when the waveform jumps in volume, producing a click. If your loop is clicking, locate the click by looping the separate sections and muting the run-in on the offending wave. If this damages the sound of the original loop too much, it's probably best to load in the loop afresh and reslice it.

You now have a sliced break. You're probably already aware of the bar measurements on your sequencer. These are your friends. A looped slice will generally be in time if it falls on a set line.

Obviously, the type of organisation that you employ on your looping will depend on the requirements of the song or remix on which you're working, but here are some basic tricks.

Below is a simple break, ready sliced…

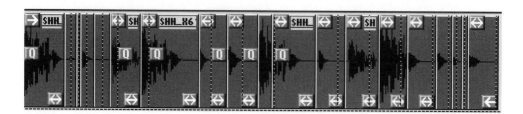

…and here's a simple pause. Just mute a section for a hip-hop "jump".

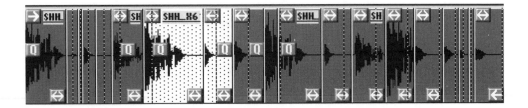

End roll. Copy the snare at maximum and quantise in the last fourth.

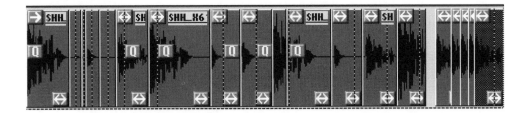

Here's the Richard D James shuffle. No need for groove control – just knock out fourths, fifths or sixths. Alternatively, you can do the reverse and double them up.

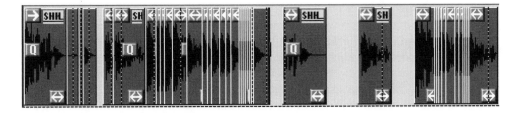

This is serious mashing. Feel free to try your own. Abstract grooves are good, clean, family fun. Sticking a mashed break on every fourth bar is a good cure for repetitive-loop syndrome.

Just because a loop is in a slow tempo, this doesn't mean that you have to keep working to that same tempo. A 100bpm hip-hop loop will loop just fine at 200bpm (or, if it's been ReCycled, at pretty much any speed). A faster bpm means more versatility, allowing you to create extremely chaotic rolls and dashes over an apparently slow drumbeat. This tempo-twisting means that Aphex Twin-speed jumps become almost easy. (Note the "almost" there!)

how to **REMIX**

a note from The Herbaliser

Jake Werry, "The Herbaliser", has his own method of working: "Blowing my own trumpet, I must claim to be one of the first to be a true sample chopper. Now I use ReCycle all of the time, but I don't rely on the chop points that ReCycle sets. Most of the time, I chop the sample by inserting my own chop points, and most of this chopping is based on the way I used to chop by hand on my Akai S1000. But, oh yes, do we chop!

"In the old days, I always liked to chop up my samples – usually I chop a bar into at least four parts, if not eight – and so I would sit for hours at my S1000 manually splicing my beats and loops into individual hits. Then, in 1996, I got a PowerPC 7600, which I upgraded to a 200MHz 604e card, and we started to use ReCycle. Like, wow! A software that literally did a job that would take about ten minutes in seconds. So we used ReCycle without using the Rexx export option for a few years, and now I have 16 outputs on my MOTU [Mark Of The Unicorn] soundcard. We have the option of sending samples as Rexx files, etc, straight to audio. So, depending on what I imagine we are going to do with a sample, from Recyle I will either send it by SCSI back to a sampler – usually drums – or I will send it as an audio Rexx file in Cubase."

vocal manipulation

Although a lot of remixes will require you to retain the original vocal line, some of the best reworkings mutate the vocals into sounds that are seriously removed from the way they appear in the original recordings. The technique of processing vocals can be divided into two methods: external (or layered) processing and direct processing. External processing relies on the addition of effects and doesn't change the original waveform, while direct processing changes the actual form of the audio. Filters, pitch-shifting and slicing all fall into this category. For a comprehensive explanation of the uses of effects and vocal tricks, have a look at Chapter 10, "Effected?". In this chapter, I'll concentrate on the direct-processing method.

For the most hands-on control, my favourite technique is to import large sections of the vocal line into ReCycle, or a similar program. Slice the vocal into sections as thinly as possible and export these sections to a sampler. ReCycle automatically creates a sample bank when it exports sections, and you can then assign the bank's pitch-shift control to a filter, giving you real-time filter control. Because of the triggering method used, you can treat the MIDI maps in your sequencer as sliced audio and can thus copy and paste sections together.

64

Sampler Settings

Sampler: My A3000 via MIDI+SCSI

Name: My A3000 via MIDI+SCSI **Rename...**	**Type:** Yamaha A3000 via MIDI+SCSI
MIDI In: MIDISport	
MIDI Out: MIDISport	
SysEx ID: 1	**Required OS:** V2.00
SCSI Bus: SCSI Manager 4.3 [None/unk...	**Found OS:** Unknown
SCSI ID: 0: ???	**Notes:** Remember to turn off the MIDI Bulk Protect switch before Transmitting to the A3000!
✗ **Verify** Check that sampler is on-line.	

Audio-slicing in ReCycle

Depending on the size of the slices, it's possible to actually rephrase an entire vocal line. Simply move the MIDI notes into the pattern you want and, as if by magic, your sampler does the work for you, creating a fresh (if not sometimes comprehensible) vocal part.

As the sampler will act as pitch-shifter, you can also drop lines and create chords of vocals, etc.

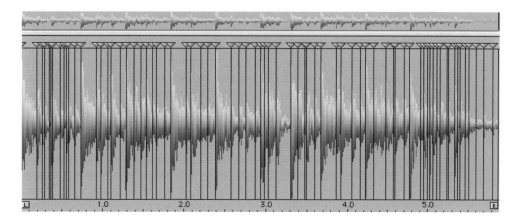

Exporting to a sampler in ReCycle

Once a certain amount of rephrasing and filter-pushing has been performed, use the sampler's Resample function to start again, this time using the already processed vocals as the sample. After you've resampled, the process can then be repeated. Try altering different filters, lowering the pitches of waves and introducing vocal rolls by employing the same method as you would on a drum loop. (You can also get the classic e-e-e-eighties stutter, but this is purely an unfortunate coincidence.) For a demonstration of serious vocal processing, listen to BT's 'Movement In Still Life', where a serious amount of sampling and resampling was used to layer together totally unsingable parts.

instruments

As with drums and the kinds of audio mentioned earlier, cut your waveforms as tightly as possible. Try creating frequency rolls and pulses, chords and sustains. Repeat the vocal process for a phrase from the song you're remixing, ReCycle it and then trigger it from your sampler. The final process you use will depend on how drastic your version is.

auto-tuners

Auto-tuners are available in both hardware and software forms and are designed to provide a solution for singers having a bad day. They can be of great help in tightening a mix. Auto-tuners calculate the original pitches of sounds (which limits their uses to monophonic sources) and use real-time pitch-shifting techniques to match the notes in a scale defined by the user. The pitch is changed by a controllable slider, allowing for very smooth, "natural" changes in pitch, although it can be sped up to achieve dramatic effects. (It's been said that the famous vocoder chorus used in the song that relaunched Cher's career, 'Believe', was achieved by using an auto-tuner set to an extremely fast speed and an appropriate scale.) An auto-tuner is obviously a valuable tool in the hands of a remixer and will provide you with more freedom to play with the original samples. And, of course, it also means that you too can have the voice of Dane Bowers.

It's not as easy to get away with changing the pitches of vocals than with changing an instrument, in terms of remixing, as a vocal line with poor timbre will always annoy the band's singer. You also risk causing a "chipmunk" effect or, worse still, the personification of sub-bass. In most cases, although it takes more time and effort, it's best to shape the song to the vocal pitch by shifting the necessary instruments.

your best friend the sampler and its manipulative world

"Without deviation, progress is not possible."
Frank Zappa

Samplers are more than just machines for looping beats and playing multisamples. Modern samplers are powerful, stand-alone sound-generating devices with their own range of effects (the newest range of Yamahas have an astounding 93 effects) and a huge degree of sound-manipulating potential. Obviously, the best way of realising your sampler's potential is through experimentation. It can be a daunting process to get to grips with a high-end sampler, but listed here are some tricks that you should be able to perform when your sampler is fresh out of the box.

reverse your sound

Probably one of the first features with which the owner of a sampler will experiment is the Reverse function. Breakbeat is littered with the reverse intro, and with this function even Disney could create oppressive dialogue of which David Lynch would be proud. Press a button and Bob's talking to midgets through your headphones! The Reverse function is also useful for turning sounds with sharp attacks and long decays into accents and fills for that essential dance mix. You can play it with more subtlety, though. For example, try reversing a looped sound (either percussive or ambient) and mix this in with the original, crossfading as mentioned earlier, in the section about looping in Chapter 6, or layering by assigning two samples to one part. Try recording a sample with a tempo delay and then reverse it. The result is closer to the dark noises in your head than you might expect.

With stereo samples of ambient or melodic sounds, try reversing one channel for a more unusual stereo image. You can also play around with panning, perhaps crossfading each one over to the other side of the stereo spectrum as they play.

Some samplers have a function that allows them to play a sample forwards automatically and then go into reverse. With rhythmic loops and percussive sounds, this can be a great way of creating some unusual effects. If your sampler doesn't offer this function (although the majority of new models do), it's a simple task to create it yourself. First, copy your sample, then reverse it and stitch it onto the back end of the original sample. If you steal the midsection of a loop when this function is activated, you can create a nice fresh loop. (Some EMUs and the recent Yamahas will do this automatically with their Remix Loop function.) Try dropping the reversed element down a semitone or two to create a pseudo-Doppler effect.

creating your own effects

Some strange and often unnatural-sounding effects can be achieved by sampling creatively. Bear this in mind when yet another boring, overdriven guitar loop becomes the centre of your remix. Simple flanger and phasing effects can be achieved by double- or triple-triggering the same sample. Rob Playford, producer of Goldie's seminal album *Timeless*, found that, by triggering hard-panned copies of the same beat milliseconds apart, a soaring flanger effect was produced. It also created a huge stereo space that you'll recognise if you've listened to Goldie's work. Alternatively, to obtain a chorus effect, use the same technique but detune the second and/or third sample by a tiny amount.

A useful trick which works well for pads and string sounds involves modulation. Try making copies of the same sample and then apply different vibrato rates to each one to create a chorus effect. Sampling at the lowest bandwidth possible on your sampler will give a good lo-fi crunch. Try deliberately sampling at too low a level and then repeatedly using the Normalising function to pump the volume back up again. Unfortunately, you'll find that your pristine sample soon gets mucked up with all kinds of digital silage. A superb way of achieving Faultline-style harmonics is to give rhythm loops extra crunch by over-normalising them, so that the peaks are clipped. Use this technique sparingly, however, as it can easily be misconstrued as sloppy mixing.

Contrary to what you might think, a bad loop can often serve as an effective production tool. With more atmospheric loops, it can actually be quite effective to have the sample gradually (or even dramatically) drifting out of time with the main rhythm. This is great for disturbing people on comedowns, especially if you increase the master reverb as the syncopation increases. You could even try deliberately running two versions of the same loop together, with one triggered regularly on the bar and the other trimmed to fall, say, a 32nd note short of the full bar, which would mean that the rhythm and melody would only be in sync once every 32 bars. This is seriously unnerving if it catches the listener unaware, but also seriously confusing if performed clumsily. Naturally, unless you're deliberately trying to send your listeners into an early bath of liquid psychosis, this technique is probably best confined to background ambient sounds rather than the more in-your-face drum loops. Pan the two samples to opposite sides of the stereo spectrum for added spatial freakiness.

extra percussion

Samplers are governed by simple mathematical principles. In fact, I'm sure that many macrocosmic revelations have been had by over-tired producers trying to work out how to use a new sampler. For example, if a sample is mapped to C1 and you play C2, as well as being an octave higher, the sample will be double the tempo of the original. Playing keys an octave apart with a drum loop will give you a plinky, double-time percussion over your original loop. The results are more unpredictable with melodic loops, but by playing around with the intervals you can come up with some interesting arpeggio-style sequences. You can even get away with using fourths for some loops and even smaller intervals, if you're looking for syncopated strangeness.

give me control

Samplers with MIDI-velocity implementation (which these days is nearly all of them) also allow you to assign other parameters to MIDI velocity (and, indeed, to other continuous controllers, such as the pitch-bend wheel, in conjunction with vocal manipulation). Here are some suggestions of ways in which you could make your samples sound more dynamic.

Assignable Tips

Try assigning the filter cut-off point to Velocity so that, when you play harder, the sound doesn't just get louder, it also gets brighter. This is a valuable effect when you're playing a sample of the original song in real time over your remix, as it gives the effect of a wave of the first song undulating under your remix. You can also try this trick with other parameters, such as pan position, which can make a staccato snare fill move across the stereo field as it gets louder. A sampler with built-in effects may allow you to assign internal effects to Velocity so that the sound becomes more (or less) affected at higher velocities. A bonus of being able to assign velocity values is that it makes samplers more pleasurable to play, and sounds which are nicer to play mean more time playing on them, therefore more time spent recording the remix and, theoretically, a better remix.

As mentioned in the previous chapter, in the section on "Vocal Manipulation", modern samplers allow you to lift large sections of audio. A finely sliced verse assigned to filter control, pitch shift and effects can almost stand alone as a remix by itself. Also, don't restrict full-blown mashing to vocals; a piano line, and even a synth part, can produce wonderfully twisted results.

Out of preference, I tend to assign filters to any available knobs. I was reared on a Groovebox and I take comfort in using knob-twisting envelope controls. Some samplers actually allow you to assign MIDI control to their own knobs.

tempo-jumping

Fine-slicing already allows you to dramatically alter tempo, but what about real-time drops and falls? For this, a standard MIDI pitch-shifter works nicely. For added control, work out the beats per minute and assign the pitch-shifter's octave for exactly half and exactly double (ie if your phrase is at 100bpm, give your pitch-shifter a range of an octave, so that one turn to the left drops the sample to 50bpm while a turn to the right boosts it to 200bpm. Both will play in time with your 100bpm sequence.) If you try this technique with ReCycled or finely sliced loops, you can achieve leaps in tempo that don't change in pitch.

Another fact that's often overlooked is that pitch shifters are assignable. Try setting the Effects option to Wet or BPM Filters. Control is power.

chapter 8

how can I fit that in?

"You are an ant."
Harvey Bear

changing the audio to fit the tempo

Central to the art of remixing is the incorporation of existing samples into a new piece of music. Tempo clashes will be a common obstacle for any remixer, especially when transforming a monged indie head-wobbler into a four-to-the-floor chart-threatener. Modern digital recording offers a few solutions to this problem, primarily time-stretching and pitch-shifting. By combining these tools – which are offered as part of most contemporary sequencers – with a modern sampler, it's possible to control almost any level of pitch and tempo.

time-stretching

Time-stretching is a facility that's found on most sequencers, and if yours doesn't have one then be assured that a plug-in will be available. With most programs, you select the audio sample and call up the Time Stretch command (usually in the Audio Function menu). Then input the original tempo and the target tempo in the appropriate boxes, time-stretch and play.

The process of time-stretching demands a serious amount of number-crunching from your computer. The basic principle, however, is relatively simple – the computer analyses the samples that comprise an audio loop, positions them on a new time grid and then resamples them.

If you increase the tempo, the computer squeezes the individual samples closer together, while in slowing the tempo the computer does the opposite, adding space between the parts. When this remapping takes place, however, the data retains the original pitch. The theory behind pitch-shifting is similar to the operation of ReCycle – ie dividing a loop and respacing it accordingly. The only drawback to time-stretching is the degree to which you can actually alter the speed. For example, a 180bpm drum loop does have a tendency to become stuttered at 100bpm. One solution (although not a foolproof one) is to use ReCycle, which inserts smaller samples extracted from the original as a sort of sound filler. The other technique is to rely on your sampler.

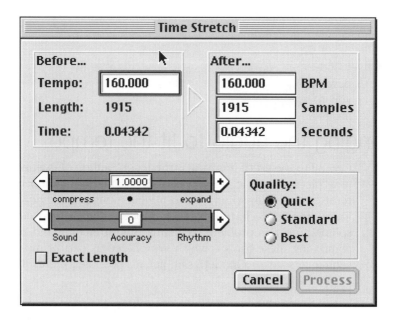

A typical time-stretch dialog box

pitch-shifting

This is certainly a technique you'll need if you intend to pursue a career in remixing. A pitch-shifter does exactly what it says on the tin: it allows you to change the pitch of the original sound without altering the speed. It works by breaking up the sound into very small pieces which are sped up or slowed down accordingly and either looped or truncated (depending on whether the sample is moving up or down in pitch) before being joined back together. The process of changing the pitch also results in a change in timbre, which becomes more exaggerated the more extreme the shift in pitch. (This is the sound of Oxide And Neutrino and our beloved Captain Kirk's nightmare: "Yourrr sooonnn isss deeaad.") This alteration in timbre can be used as an effect, but if you're just trying to fit a sample to a certain key then it can prove frustrating. Offline pitch-shifters are better than real-time models, but to be true to the original sound you can only afford to effect a few notches of adjustment. Samplers map samples to keys in a very similar way.

Pitch-shifting was actually developed with samplers in mind. When a sample is assigned to a fixed key on a keyboard, if any other key is played then the pitch and the speed of the sample is changed to match the note being played. Playing keys higher up the keyboard speeds up the tempo and pitch, while the opposite is true of playing lower keys. Pitch-shifting gives you the ability to speed up the tempo on your sampler and then pitch the sample down to its original note. Although this process is far more time consuming than time-stretching, it can sometimes yield higher-quality results. Roland's newest sampler will actually perform this function automatically, allowing you to change the key without also changing the speed or timbre – an impressive feature, reflected in the device's price. But hopefully, with this technology becoming more available, prices will fall respectively. Until that time, the manual process outlined above is available to all.

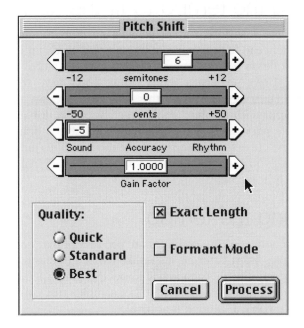

A typical pitch-shift dialog box

Time-stretching can be a serious creative device. Classic jungle and some trip-hop thrive off stretched grooves. Be careful, though, as, if you stretch a sound too much, you end up with all kinds of weird results as the sampler struggles to make sense of it all. While this isn't so good if you're going for hyper-accurate sampling in your remix, it can be seen as a route to mangling heaven. Remember: if in doubt, experiment. Even if you want the sound at its original pitch, try time-stretching it, recording it to tape, resampling it and then shrinking it back down to the original length. What gets lost in the translation may just work to your advantage.

An alternative to time-stretching an entire rhythm loop is to use the pitch-bend wheel to stretch parts of the loop just enough to make it fit to a new tempo. Of course, the sample will change in pitch somewhere along the line, but this can give a happy creative result. (Listen to some old jungle music to hear what I mean.) It takes a bit of trial and error to get right, but if you record the movement of the pitch-bend wheel as part of a MIDI sequence, you'll be able to fine-tune it so that the bent rhythm fits the new tempo exactly. You can also use this to create jumps in tempo or achieve beat mangling as sections change into each other.

changing the tempo to fit the audio

The most obvious way of achieving this is to simply change your MIDI sequence to fit the tempo of the samples used in the original song. This can be done on your sequencer by changing the global tempo, inputting a new one. Unfortunately, a remix often won't have the same tempo as the original song. However, this isn't to say that difference lies only in discrepancies in bpm; audio rearrangement, for example, will be on the whole performed at the original speed, and a dramatically different song can be created without launching the bpm into jungle territory. Of course, unless you already know the tempo of the original sample, this process is purely academic.

calculating the tempo

Depending on your commission, you may or may not have the bpms of your samples listed. After all, it's unlikely that a traditional guitar band who have recorded directly to tape will know the exact speed of their song. If this is the case, you'll have a DAT full of samples that could be at any speed. But don't worry, a solution is at hand.

Most sequencers will calculate tempo for you. The way in which they do this varies from sequencer to sequencer, so it's always best to consult your manual, but the general routine is that you tell the sequencer how many bars are contained in a musical event and then select a region of the sound file corresponding to that number of bars. Your sequencer will then calculate the bpm and adjust the tempo accordingly. Some sequencers don't offer this facility, however, and sometimes time is of the essence. In these cases, it's possible to work out the tempo manually. I personally prefer this method, as it's more hands-on and comes with the added advantage of allowing you to determine bar length.

The process is simple. Import the audio file into your sequencer and loop the number of bars required. The number of bars you'll need will depend on the length of the phrase or drum part and the feel that you want to achieve – a shorter length will give a sampler-triggered feel that's popular in big beat, while a longer length will make the phrase sound as if it's played more naturally, although it will also be harder to loop. Once you've decided on the amount of bars you need, open the Wave Editor. With practice, you should be able to identify which part of the waveform corresponds to the sound you're after, and this will help you when it comes to looping. Now just change the global tempo until the audio loops cleanly. NB: If possible, always start your loop from the beginning of the audio file, as this will mean that your loop will always start from the beginning of the phrase.

Most generic beats group into bpm categories. For reference, they are listed here as follows:

- Hip-hop/trip-hop – 80-120bpm (although trip-hop, by its nature, can vary);

- House – between 120bpm for trance, moving up to 150bpm for hard house;

- Garage – 130-140bpm;

- Drum and bass – 160-170bpm;

- Jungle – 170bpm and over;

- Electronica – 50-230bpm;

- Ambient – 0bpm-maximum;

- Breakbeat – 130-150bpm.

Of course, these are purely guidelines to give you a rough working area when looping and hopefully save you a bit of time. As always, there are no fixed rules.

syncing

OK, so you've established a tempo for your samples and you want to keep the samples at their original speeds. You now have to sync the original to the added parts. If you've cut the song and taken some hooks, triggering them from your sampler will present little or no synchronisation problems (assuming, of course, that you've trimmed and looped them correctly). Always remember to retrigger the loops every bar or so and have your sampler set to Single Play for accuracy's sake.

If you're using an entire section that's too long to sample, syncing suddenly becomes an issue. First, be sure that the audio starts exactly on the bar, as even a finely calculated tempo will sound like a SunRa hangover if you start it a bar and a half out of sync with the rest of your audio. Of course, this is irrelevant if the kind producers of the original song have sent in track sheets with the tapes. Track sheets are basically written records of the recording process noting start times, channel assignments and EQ settings, and they will make your job as a remixer much easier. Unfortunately, some are never sent, some are lost and some are never written in the first place. If your remix is missing this written history, you'll have to jiggle start times around until everything synchronises together properly. In these cases, there's no real short-cut to doing this, other than just fiddling. When it sounds right, it is right. Of course, if it proves to be a real problem, you could try building the song around the part you can't get in time instead of flying in samples at random start points.

loop turns and
clicking perfection

"The real meaning of the word 'synthetic' means 'putting together'."
Ralf Hütter, Kraftwerk

Looping is going to be central to your remixing work, and as dance music is built around loop-based production you should already be familiar with the basic principles. However, as with all basic principles, the results can be very hit and miss. Looping simple drum grooves usually presents no problem, but what about sounds that evolve over long periods, where the timbre and volume at the end of the sample can be radically different from that at the start?

When remixing ambient works or experimental soundscapes, you'll occasionally run into the need to use texture loops. Orchestrations will also need to be looped over large sections. Conventional looping (whereby a section of the sample is looped in order to conserve memory after the initial attack of the sound has passed) is not appropriate here. The aim instead is to provide a loop that uses the entire sample and cycles to infinity without sounding like a broken record. This means invoking the dreadful word *crossfading*, ie the process of merging two samples together to form a single sample. With most samplers, you have a number of options at your disposal to perform this task. However, crossfading is a seriously time-consuming business, and merging two pieces of a sample on a tiny sampler display can sometimes be as much work as mixing an entire song. Luckily, modern sequencers allow you to perform hard loops and crossfades in a hands-on way.

looping textures and orchestral chunks

Once you've loaded the source material onto your sequencer, the first thing to do is locate the region you want to loop and then cut around it, giving yourself a few extra seconds on either side. Make sure that the Tempo window of your display is measuring bars and beats and not SMPTE. When it comes to textures, the actual tempo and time signature of the material isn't critical – the bar lines merely serve as an accurate scale to help you cut segments of equal length. If the loop start point is critical, locate it and make a cut there. Then set the snap value for your Move tools to the Bar setting (the default setting on starting up) and move the cut segment to the start of a bar line, so that your sample starts exactly on the bar.

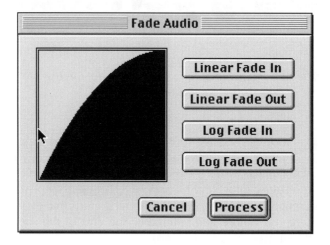

Now turn the snap value to Off, move the section preceding the cut right up to the cut itself and glue the two parts back together. Then switch the snap value back to Bar and indicate the segment you wish to loop with the left and right markers. If there's no specific place you'd like the loop to start, there's no need to perform the cut-and-move operation. Simply place markers on the bar lines that delineate the loop.

let the crossfading begin

In order to produce a decent crossfade, you'll need to create a linear fade-in from silence to full volume near the beginning of the section you wish to loop and a linear fade-out from full volume to silence near the end of the section. You can do this by highlighting the relevant part and selecting the appropriate fade from the Audio Function menu in your sampler. How rapid you make these fades will depend on the nature of the material you're looping, although there are two important points to note: firstly, the fades must be of the same duration at either end; and secondly, the start and end of the section you wish to loop must come exactly halfway through the fades you make, however long you decide the fades should be.

First of all, cut the audio up into three chunks, so that you can apply the fades to the chunks at either end without affecting the middle section. Then apply a linear fade-in to the first chunk, leave the central chunk as it is and apply a linear fade-out to the third chunk. (Take care when cutting orchestral chunks, as even the most carefully faded string sustain sounds wrong as it fades over three entire octaves.)

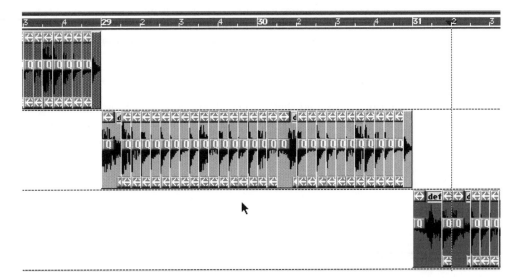

Next, copy all three chunks onto another track and move the copied set of chunks so that the first chunk, with the fade-in, exactly overlaps the fade-out chunk of the original set. (Remember, the fade-in has to be the same length as the fade-out, so this shouldn't be too difficult.) Then repeat the process a third time. You'll now have three sets of triplets of chunks and each set will be crossfaded into the next. At this point, you can audition the crossfades to make sure that there's a smooth, inaudible transition from the end of one set of the three chunks to the start of the next. (The Crossfade function will be hidden in the Audio Functions menu, the Options menu or in the toolbar.) If you're happy with the result, position the left and right markers so that the left marker falls halfway through the fade-in of the second set of the three chunks and the right marker falls halfway through the fade-out on the same set.

It's also possible to loop in the middle set of the three chunks. Provided that all of the pan, volume and EQ settings are the same for both tracks, the way in which the material has been copied will ensure that the audio to the right of the left marker sounds exactly the same as everything to the right of the right marker. So, if you now digitally merge the material from both tracks between the two markers, you'll have a section that will play seamlessly into a copy of itself, since the beginning is an exact copy of what follows the end. In other words, it will loop perfectly.

Now you can export your crossfade as a single audio file, either directly into your sampler or into a program like ReCycle. If used carefully, ReCycle can work just as well with textures and melody as with drum loops. (It does negate dramatic tempo change, but it is possible.) Sometimes a dramatic change in the speed of a melody is central to a remix, so it pays to experiment.

troubleshooting

When trimming a sample that's going to be used as a loop, you can give yourself a helping hand by pitching the sample down one or even two octaves. Slowing down a loop makes it much easier to find the "right" start and end points. Then, when you've finished, just put the loop back up to the correct tempo/pitch.

If the transition between loops sounds too abrupt, make the fades longer, while ensuring that you keep the left and right markers in the middle of their respective fades. The longer the fade chunks, the more material on either side of the left and right markers will be incorporated into the final sample, so the resulting loop will sound less like the original source material. This is sometimes a boon in terms of remix serendipity, but it's just as often something that's worth smoothing out.

If the volume still seems uneven across the loops, try experimenting with different fade-in and fade-out curves, using a convex curve for the fade-in and its inverse shape for the fade-out. If your sequencer doesn't offer extensive fade-editing, try playing with the length of the section you're fading. Is it unloopable? You may wish to loop a section of music which isn't a whole number of seconds long, and so using 120bpm as a grid won't give an accurate stop point. By increasing the bpm of your time axis, you can home in on the source material with more accuracy, since you have more bar lines over a given period. However, this is still hit and miss. Better still, if you have a Compute Tempo facility, place the markers at the start and end of the section you want to loop and tell the program that this section is so many bars long. Then cut and move the section to the start of one of the new bar lines and repaste the preceding section, as before. You're now ready to make bar-accurate cuts, which should allow you to loop everything, even oddly timed samples and phrases that clearly weren't intended for looping. This same technique can also be used to create new sounds and phrases, which can be very useful when approaching an experimental remix. Try crossfading a vocal line with a keyboard part or a synth line with a bass.

Once you're adept at crossfading, you'll be able to produce huge, evolving melodies taken from original songs, deep pads that metamorphose into lead vocals or a whole song that transforms into an orchestral work-out. This need not be limited to individual parts, and there's nothing to stop you sampling the end portion of your finished remix and mutating it into a solo melody.

You could also make complex drones and animated ambient washes, making an entire ambient remix that, although totally removed from the original, is made entirely of the original's ingredients. If you're sampling wholesale from a track, looping in this way will stop your loops from sounding stilted, without the abrupt change as the sample jumps from the end of the loop to its beginning.

loops and crossfades for rhythm

Using crossfades to loop samples with rhythmic elements is much more hazardous than trying to loop non-rhythmic sounds and phrases. If you try to loop sections without paying attention to the tempo of the source material, a bar on the grid will almost certainly not be a bar in reality. You might get a result that seems to stay in time with itself, but it's more than likely that it will create a loop with an incomplete bar at the end, or there will be interference at the crossfade, with completely mismatched beats. When it comes to working with rhythmic material, I recommend that you always find out the tempo, by using either of the techniques I've described here. Even when the correct tempo has been found, if the rhythm hasn't been played with metronomic accuracy, you may get flaws in the crossfades. Many studios insist that a drummer plays to a click track, but drummers are human and so are prone to error. (Many jokes could be inserted here, but it's best if you just picture a drummer you know and smile quietly to yourself.) With dance music – created with time clocks, quantising and visual perfection – you should have no trouble in calculating a house beat, but if you're remixing a guitar band then you're far more likely to discover metronomic discrepancies. If this happens, reduce the crossfade size to as little as the length of a crotchet (quarter note). As long as you use a small amount of overlap, you'll still retain some of the natural decay and reverb of the sound at the end of the sample, avoiding the abrupt changes that can occur when you make loops without employing crossfades.

Another short-cut is to isolate the offending snare or cymbal and play it in time using MIDI and a single sample. Just cut the loop short and program the end with the individual hits. Sample the whole loop direct from your sequencer and repeat the whole process. Crossfading drum loops is a good technique to use if you want to avoid the bar-triggered sequence sound that is synonymous with dance. If you use fade breaks and central rhythm, you can come close to simulating a real drummer. (Note the use of the word "close" – only a real drummer is a capable of real drumming, but with a combination of programming, looping and blind experimenting, you can come just that little bit closer.)

chapter 10

effected?

"I like sound-effect records. Sometimes, late at night, I get a mint julep and just sit there and listen to sound effects. I'm surprised there aren't more of them in the charts."
    Bob Dylan

n this section we'll look at some of the more common types of effects and their uses. Effects are some of the most often-used but little-understood tools of a producer. If you find that your current remix project seems to be lacking in something, stripping away all the outboard and plug-in effects will give the track its missing edge, more often than not. This isn't to say that effects aren't an invaluable form of transforming sound, however. After all, remixing is about altering an original to turn it into something else. Effects themselves do exactly this – they take an original sound and change it.

reverb

Reverb is definitely the most common effect, and almost all sound units, samplers and sequencers will have at least one type. It's used to a greater or lesser extent in all recordings and is an incredibly useful tool, yet it is often the case that poor use of reverb can ruin an otherwise great mix.

Reverb provides depth and a sense of space. Ambient music uses great washes of it to conjure up the picture of a flock of geese in the distance or fighting pensioners down the hall. The basic reverb unit comes in three types of processing format: digital, plate and spring. Each type offers its own sound, but the most common reverb units in use today are digital, and it's this variety that you'll find in your sequencer plug-ins.

reverb tips

The most common mistake with reverb is simply using too much. Putting a lot of reverb on a mix creates a muddy and unprofessional sound – not a good way to impress your client. As with EQ, instead of adding reverb to define one part, try taking some away from other parts. The effect can be far more dramatic, and it will leave you with a clean mix. Another thing to watch out for is using digital reverb on low frequencies, which can sometimes lead to distortion. Here are some nice creative uses of reverb.

Weird Stereo Noise Gate

- Send the desired sound from the mixer via an auxiliary (echo/effects) send to the reverb unit.
- Bring the left and right outputs from the reverb unit into the left and right inputs of a stereo noise gate.
- Set the Reverb setting to a large reverb setting, such as a hall.
- Set the gate to Stereo mode, with a low threshold and a fast attack.
- Next, set a short decay time on the gate and then send the reverb through. You should get a massive reverb sound which, by adjusting how long the gates stay open, cuts out quickly.
- You can now mash up the sound by changing the gate's attack time.

The beauty of doing it yourself is that you can get just the correct amount of open/hold time on the gate in order to obtain the sound you're after, and you can tailor the result to rhythmically fit the song. Most cheaper reverb units with gated reverb fix the decay time, which can clash rhythmically with the song. Of course, almost all digital units offer MIDI sync, but don't rely entirely on technology. Some nice effects can be obtained via manual manipulation, and you can actually create your own rhythmic reverbs.

Rhythmic Reverb

Set the gates to Fixed Stereo mode and Trigger Input mode. Then, while having the reverb signal go through them, program the gates to open and close rhythmically with something like a hi-hat pattern. This is incredibly useful when changing individual samples to fit a remix's new bpm, while extreme use of this method creates an almost vocoder-ish sound.

To trigger the effect, send a rhythm part to the trigger input socket from an aux send. Alternatively, with an insert cable plugged into the appropriate channel, you can use the insert socket.

Reverse Reverb

Have you ever wondered how BT and Chicane achieve a reverse reverb that comes before the actual vocal line? Well, so have I, and although I've never had the chance to ask them how they do it, this seems to be the method they've used.

- First, choose a reverb with a fairly long decay.
- Next, apply some to your vocal line, synth or snare drum.
- Play the song and route the reverb into the soundcard only, recording only the reverb.
- Line up the reverb with the vocal, synth or drum and apply a Reverse Audio command.
- You will now have a reversed reverb part that you can drag around in relation to the original sound until you arrive at a cool effect.

Unlike effects derived from units that have a "reverse reverb" patch, this one really does play before the original sound. Try this on vocals or guitar riffs for soaring trance effects.

Offset Reverb

With computer sequencing, you can record a reverb from, say, a synth or a vocal part onto an audio channel and then drag it around to offset it in time from the original. But why stop there? You can also copy the reverb over to an adjacent channel and then offset each reverb signal from the original sound by a different amount. Once you have a result that you like, crossfade the parts together. (For help with this, see the previous chapter.) This means that you can get single-, double- or triple-offset reverb, or whatever your sequencer will allow.

Atmospheric Reverb

You can also create your own atmospherics. If you have an old spring-reverb unit, you can rip off the casing and shout into the springs. You probably won't hear the result while you're doing it, but if you record it onto your sampler this method can create some superb atmospheric noises. An effect that sounds similar to Brian Eno sitting in a tin elevator can be achieved by slightly shaking the reverb box as you scream. You can also try running different objects up and down the springs and recording this, while simply tapping or banging the unit produces some distinctly unsettling noises, especially if you run the sound through a normal reverb unit or onboard effects.

Effects like these will create more interesting sounds in your tunes than buying a massive top-end synth. The beauty of DIY tricks is that they are never repeatable. The scream in C that you perform will be one of a kind, unavailable on any synth.

Over-Applied Reverb

Another nice effect which is currently running the risk of becoming clichéd is that of absolutely drenching a guitar in the biggest hall or canyon setting you can find. With this effect, what was once a guitar becomes, in my opinion, something really sublime. However, if you added this amount of reverb to your mix, it would swamp every other part. Instead, try sampling a small portion and loop it. (It may need to be crossfaded.) If you have access to a guitar, I strongly recommend multisampling, since using the pads achieves a really nice Mogwai atmosphere. In a remix, you can cut up a guitar part into its composite chords and use this technique to play the melody underneath the original – instant depth and Glasgow grandeur!

compression

Compressors are found in every studio in the country. Basically, a compressor automatically adjusts and maintains the signal levels of sounds, evening out the distance between loud and quiet parts by crushing and raising audio in relation to its original level. Compression is used on all commercial tracks these days and helps to create the radio sheen we are all used to. R&B, garage and pop music all have the life crunched out of them by heavy compression applied on parts, as well as on the overall mix. If a song sounds like it's made of a condensed, paper-thin sheet of titanium (not tinny but heavy), you can be fairly certain that a compressor made an entrance at some point in the recording chain.

Compression was originally invented to allow records to be pressed more easily. Vinyl only allows for a certain depth of groove before the needle begins to skip. Old pressing centres couldn't accommodate low-end bass, and so some sound technicians developed compression in order to allow records to have low frequencies without causing the needle to skip all over the place. From its early days, it has developed into an essential tool for producers, enabling them to create phat, punchy bass lines and polished audio peaks.

Compressors come in two main flavours, hard-knee and soft-knee, while some variations in taste and texture can be obtained with some valve compressors and Supernice compression, which is a brand rather than a sound. Various other systems tend to operate in the middle ground of hard- and soft-knee compression, although hard-knee compression is the type that you'll find on most standard units. If you're using a normal compressor, nothing will happen until the threshold is breached. When that happens, the compression cuts in.

Let's say you've set a compression ratio of 4:1. Once the threshold is passed, the compressor allows only 1dB of increase in signal level at the output for every 4dB rise in input signal level above the threshold setting. So, for future reference, the first number on a compressor refers to trigger volume and the second to the level of limiting. On a hard-knee compressor, this full amount of compression (as set by the ratio) is applied in full as soon as the input level rises above the threshold.

Soft-knee compressors, however, work differently, applying compression gradually as the signal approaches the threshold level. As the input signal gets within about 10dB of the threshold level, the soft-knee compressor starts to apply compression gently, but with a very low ratio, which increases proportionally as the input level gets nearer to the threshold setting so that, by the time the input level actually reaches the threshold level, the compressor is applying its gain reduction at the full level, as set by the ratio control. Soft-knee compressors are thus more subtle, as they don't wait around doing nothing and then suddenly apply the full level of compression at the threshold point.

Soft-knee modules are softer in use, and are thus more suitable for compressing whole mixes or gentler sounds that hover around the threshold point. Some units allow you to switch between hard- and soft-knee functions, while others offer only one type of compression.

As with practically all audio hardware, compressors are also available in software form, either as a plug-in or as a separate program. Mastering software usually offers at least one type of compression, and there's a good chance that your sampler has a compression function hidden deep in its effects banks.

The table of settings below is a rough guideline for compressing sounds. Don't be afraid to experiment, however, as heavily compressed audio can sometimes be wonderful at emulating filters and distance.

Sound	Attack	Release	Ratio	Hard/Soft	Gain Reduction
Vocal	fast	0.5 seconds	2:1-8:1	soft	3-8dB
Loud vocal	fast	0.3 seconds	4:1-10:1	hard	5-15dB
Acoustic guitar	5-10ms	0.5 seconds	5:1-10:1	soft/hard	5-15dB
Electric guitar	2-5ms	0.5 seconds	8:1-10:1	hard	5-15dB
Kick and snare	1-3ms	0.2 seconds	5:1-10:1	hard	5-15dB
Bass	1-10ms	0.5 seconds	4:1-12:1	hard	5-15dB
Mix	fast	0.4 seconds	2:1-6:1	soft	2-10dB
General (Stereo link on)	fast	0.5 seconds	5:1	soft	2-10dB

Creatively, the obvious way to use a compressor unit is to hideously overpower it, creating fat chunks of rhythm at which even an obese Mexican gun salesman will tremble, while soft overlay will widen string and orchestral parts. If your original song has a limp drum loop, you can put it in touch with a good steroid dealer by applying a little hard-knee consideration. Arriving at a punchy, hard attack to use on drum loops and bass lines is a simple procedure, and the signature bass that kicks through the mix on garage records can be achieved in this way. To achieve this, set up your compressor on a snare drum, for example, and simply set a slower attack time – somewhere in the region of 1-5ms. This allows the initial fast attack of the snare or bass to bust through before the compressor kicks in to crush the sound.

delay

Can you remember crawling across the room to Roger Waters' echoing scream as he tries to warn someone called Eugene about carpentry tools? Or have you marvelled, mid disco, at the infinite note sustain of The Edge? Well, you can rest assured that neither man has alien powers. Just a delay box.

Delay is basically echo and is used a great deal in modern recording. However, if you don't have a vast knowledge of its attributes, it's an effect that, while making The Edge appear as a lesser-known angel, will leave your tempos confused and the samples you're trying to remix drowning in their own infinities.

As with reverb, there are a number of different units available: tape, analogue and digital. Tape and analogue units each have distinctive sounds, with analogue units being similar to digital but harsher and metallic in sound and tape units giving you that old '70s dub-plate sound, which is excellent for feedback.

There are two types of digital delay: those with knobs and those without. Each type will perform certain jobs better than the other. (OK, this gives me a chance to mention something about not having to be knobless any more, but I'll let it pass.) There are some delay effects that both types of unit will provide, and cheap, feature-packed delays are now readily available from most music shops.

So, what do you want to with your delay? Well, a good first attempt is a static timed delay (tempo delay). The static timed delay is what makes any style of dance tune flow. It makes your beats and synth lines roll in a really fluid way and is essential for dub. Also, timing your delay can make a lifeless vocal line rise in the mix. Alternatively, you could create a swing beat by simply dropping timed delay on the downbeat. Snare rolls and fluid rises can also be achieved by applying delay on single parts, which can save you hours in programming time if you're trying to get fluid, funky beats, synth lines or racy beats and lines. Timed delay will also often create cross-rhythms that you would never have thought of with loops in mind.

When remixing, try applying a tempo delay to the original mix of the song. The results can sometimes show you where to take a piece of music. Beware, though, that simply adding delay could make a seriously shoddy remix.

The tempo-delay effect is available as an effect plug-in, but making your own is a simple procedure. Send a click track at a given bpm to the delay unit and then adjust the delay time until you get a cool cross-rhythm. Once you've got some nice extra percussion and depth, try punching a channel in and out and just listen to the rhythmic delay wind off into the distance. This is the sound of dub.

Another thing you can do is bring the delay back through a spare channel on the desk and add reverb to it. To play on the dub feel, create some feedback at breakdowns by turning up the send and return – instant, real-time feedback is at your fingertips. Meanwhile, a nice feedback effect can be achieved by using an old analogue guitar pedal. (Actually, a digital pedal can achieve a similar effect, but the harsh rises in volume can cause some nasty tweeter-destroying distortion.) Route the pedal between your sampler and your sequencer. You should then be able to route individual samples, depending on your sampler's output sockets. First, get a nice tempo delay rolling, and then, when the urge takes you, boost all of the controls to maximum. This makes the sample echo back onto itself, rising in feedback as the speed of the delay increases. Eventually, your sample will become a whirling rising tone that implodes on itself. This technique is used by Graham Coxon on Blur's album *13*, and you'll also find it in a lot of early psychedelia. This trick is great for inserting vocal snippets into a remix, since you have real-time control over their swirling destruction. Try layering tiny snippets over the original vocal for a major phrase remix.

To make your samples sound like they're echoing in a tin bucket, set a short delay time – around 100ms – and then set the feedback to about 50-60 per cent, or whatever is right for you. (Note that this method works only with digital delay units.) Tweak a send to the delay unit from the sampler and you'll get a rattling delay good for jungle snares and for creating lo-fi vocal or instrument phrases. You can adjust this effect by setting the modulation rate to a low setting or almost zero and the modulation depth to something higher – maybe 40-50 per cent – and the sample effect should wind up and down. Then adjust the modulation rate to match the tempo of the track so that the rise and fall times are at a speed that matches the track. This method will give you instant jungle breaks and vocals. Try using jungle-sounding effects out of the context of a frantic drumbeat and bask in the surprising warmth of the result.

With the increasing use of 360° panning, delay units can be used to emulate a seriously wide stereo field, saving you from the need to invest a serious amount of money in expensive equipment. Simply apply two separate delay units to one stereo channel, one to the left and one to the right, sending reverb in separate directions. (A short delay achieves the best results here.) This method is much easier if two delays are used or when a plug-in is paired with an outboard unit, although it's still possible to achieve the same effect with one unit – simply route the effect on one channel, record the results onto your hard drive and repeat the process for the opposite channel. When combined with chorus, this method can create double-layered pads and rock-polishing bass. Just set up the delay unit for a standard chorus sound – that is, a low delay time (about 100ms), about 20 per cent feedback, a modulation depth of about 25 per cent and a modulation rate of 50 per cent – and then pan the original synth to the left and the delay return to the right for a nice, fat, stereo-spread sound. This method also works well on backing-vocal harmonies, allowing you to spread them right across the stereo field and separate them from the main vocal. It's also extremely useful with layered vocals, and it will even help you to polish poorly recorded or tuneless singing, which is great when the hook you want for your remix behaves like stale bread when freed from the original mix.

This basically covers the main types of effects. The thing is, even abusing an antique spring reverb unit has its limitations. In the last few years, manufacturers have started to release effects units on a biblical scale, partly inspired by the DJ market and partly to keep up with musical demands. Plug-ins and effects units now provide synths with tone control and…well, basically, with the Philosopher's Stone. Equipment like Korg's Koas pad and Alesis' AirFX offer totally hands-on, real-time control. And hands-on here really does mean hands-on – the Koas pad works like a square ribbon controller, while the AirFX pad operates somewhere between theremin control and semaphore. For the remix and DJ market, these effects are particularly appealing. Remixers can now give heavily sequenced samples a fluid, "live" feel by applying huge, bpm-timed filters to entire mixes. Of course, you can also pick up a cheap multi-effects bass pedal and still get blinding results.

chapter 11

finding that frequency

"We're always searching. I think that now we're on the point of finding."
John Coltrane.

A s any producer will tell you, EQ can make or break a mix. Just as a painter will mix primary colours to accentuate certain areas of a painting and draw the eye across the canvas, so a producer will mix high, low and mid-range frequencies to achieve subtle colourings of tone that a good mix demands. Often, when you listen back to one of your mixes, two or more sounds operating in the same frequency can combine in synergy to create a new sound that's greater than the sum of its parts. This blending of sound creates new timbres and also forces sounds apart, and it's this separation of sounds that is particularly important in most dance music, as in this genre there are lots of low frequencies infringing on each other's wavelengths – bass lines and kick drums, for example. (A lot of jungle producers will pitch up their drum loops to allow low basses to sit comfortably in the mix.) The same thing applies to mid-range sounds – snares, hi-hats and bongos all tend to occupy a similar wavelength and will need to stand out from each other.

EQ can vastly affect the character of a sound but, if used subtly, can also change the presence of a sound without altering its tonal quality. This is the key to creating the spacious mixes with which we're all accustomed. Like effects, less is more, so always try and cut frequencies before boosting them.

types of EQ

Graphic Equalisers

Graphic equalisers can be found on any reasonable home stereo, and these generally comprise a series of faders labelled with various frequencies, with the lowest on the right and the highest on the left. The individual sliders have a centre setting of zero and usually provide +/-12dB of boost/cut. For the most part, however, the EQ that you'll be using to remix will be far more advanced.

High-Pass Filters

A high-pass filter allows all high frequencies to pass through it unaffected but lowers the boost of the low frequencies in accordance with their relative value. The lower they are, the stronger the cut.

Low-Pass Filters

A low-pass filter employs the same principles as a high-pass filter but in reverse – the high frequencies are rolled off, leaving the low-end sound intact.

Parametric Equalisation

This type of equalisation allows you to choose the range of frequency that you want to boost or cut, and it's this type that you'll find built into the channels in Cubase and on most sequencers. It's extremely flexible, and many rewarding and frustrating hours can be spent tweaking tiny settings. By sweeping through the frequencies, you can track down unwanted resonances and lower them by reducing their gain value, while if you need to emphasise an instrument you can find the frequency that makes it stand out and simply boost it.

There is also a control that helps you focus even more closely on a particular frequency. For example, if you set a parametric EQ to work at 1kHz, you'll usually boost a range from 500Hz to 200Hz, with 1,000Hz as the peak. This range is called the *bandwidth*. The Q control on an equaliser will alter the bandwidth that is boosted.

EQ killing

There's a lot of fan-remixed material circulating on the Internet at the moment, with MP3 DJs competing to create more outlandish versions of popular songs and fans honouring their idols by uploading tributary reworkings. There are also lots of unauthorised remixes out there, which can often be found in unmarked vans full of white-label discs. These remixes cater for the exclusive-obsessed DJs that pepper-shoot the country. In fact, many Top-Ten dance successes were originally remixes created by bored producers who owned such vans.

If a remix is unauthorised, it usually means that the record company didn't send the remixer handy original tapes and he had to isolate the samples. This technique is known as *EQ killing*. As you know, on a good mix, each part occupies its own sonic space, with as little frequency overlap as possible. By homing in on the other frequencies and "killing" them, however, it's possible to sample these individual parts and use them in isolation. This extreme use of EQ won't work on a standard mixing desk or sequencer because, relatively speaking, even parametric equalisers are quite subtle. There is some audio-ripping software out there, but it tends to be automatic and not very precise. The best way to solo audio buried in a mix is to use an outboard box. The effects manufacturer Electrix has recently devised the appropriately named EQKiller, which, as its name suggests, kills frequency bands with quite startling accuracy. The best feature, however, is real-time control, which allows you to punch out frequencies on the fly. With this device, DJs can create live remixes and producers can add another powerful filter to their set-up.

Remixing seems to be getting easier (sigh), but you still need to be able to polish sounds, which leads us to…

tonal EQing

Stuck with a vocal line that sounds like a misinformed advert for flu relief? What if the only usable guitar sample you have at your disposal still resembles a toddler's metalwork class? The best solution lies with tonal EQing.

Particular musical styles require particular approaches, but some generalisations can be made. (Again, as I have stressed throughout this book, the secret of an amazing remix is originality and experimentation. All of the below are just generalisations.) Here are some standards of EQ for you to work with. Remember that some of the samples you receive from your client may well have been EQ'd already, so it's perhaps best to lay off heavy dramatisation, unless of course this is the effect you're trying to achieve.

EQing Vocals

Usually, your safest bet is to start with the mid range for vocals, although adding boost to the top range can sometimes help to create a sense of space. Always change your EQ settings if you're tracking or using more than one set of vocals, and with backing vocals you should try to stick to the mid range, as this will allow the lead vocals to ride on top.

EQing Brass And Wind Sounds

Listen to classical music. A baritone sax is used for the bottom end – it's not just a clever name – while an alto sax occupies a toppier EQ level. Brass and other wind instruments, meanwhile, have a similar tonal quality to vocals, and so similar treatments apply, since all three need to lie on top of the overall mix.

EQing Bass Sounds

On the whole, bass sounds are the most difficult part of the mix to get right. Always try to listen to your mix over a variety of different speakers, as this will point out the vast difference in bass tone produced by different systems. Basses hog a huge range of frequencies and can sometimes destroy a mix – what sounds good on a decent set of monitors can drown an entire mix on cheaper speakers. Bass frequencies like to hug kick drums and pads, so the easiest solution is to use lots of compression to drop the very low and high ranges.

EQing String Sounds

Solo strings – especially those of the synth variety – often need to be fattened up, and adding gain to the mid range can usually accomplish this. String sections and string pads, on the other hand, tend to occupy a huge spectrum of frequencies. In such a case, your best bet is to cut frequencies, but what you cut and where you cut it will depend on the song on which you're working. After all, the resonant beating of string sounds is often used as an effect in its own right in techno and jungle. As always, the best thing to do is experiment.

EQing Piano Sounds

A big one, this, as the variety is huge. Certain piano sounds can act as trademarks for certain styles – garage pianos, for example, are typically bright or soft and jazzy, while nu-skool breaks tend to opt for a more classical sound. Hip-hop, on the other hand, can utilise any sound. Synth piano patches usually emphasise high frequencies and attack timbres but often lack the warm mid tones that are so vital for relaxed jazz meanderings. In this case, try boosting the lower mid range to bring back that natural piano sound. Conversely, if you're using a sample library and need a cheesier lead for a house track, you'll need to boost the high frequencies in order to accentuate your arpeggios.

EQing Drum Sounds

There's certainly not enough room in this entire book to outline all of the approaches to EQing drum sounds, since most producers have their own rules and preferences. Having said that, however, the kick drum tends to be the most problematic sound to EQ in dance music. As with bass sounds, try to listen to your mix on every piece of stereo equipment you have and check out the range that your particular thump occupies. With house music, increase the bottom end; with drum and bass, cut the bottom end; and with hip-hop, play with whatever suits the song best. Snare drums usually respond best to a little gain in the mid range, or you could add some gain to the high frequencies and cut the mid range in order to obtain a crisper jazz snare sound. Toms also benefit from a touch of top, which helps to pronounce their attack and adds realism to the sound, although a low-end boost will give them more presence in a mix.

The upper mid range is also where you'll find stick sounds and rides. Changing the EQ on different cymbals will give a deep texture to your drums, and panning is also useful. I usually try to mirror a real drum kit, moving the cymbals in a round pan so that each occupies its own part of the stereo spectrum.

quick tips for overall EQing

- Always listen to the whole track dry, with no effects, no EQ, nothing, as this will help you to determine where things want to sit. Of course, if the song you're remixing comes with processed samples, this can't be done, although a way around this problem is to treat the song as an original sound. Of course, this will probably influence your later use of effects. A relatively effective way of reducing effects on pre-processed samples is to use a limiter or some form of compression. You can also target the frequency band where the sample is most effected and reduce the gain there, although this can lead to unwanted tonal change.

- Thin out pads, backing vocals and acoustic-guitar parts with EQ. Perversely, this dramatises dynamics rather than diminishes them.

- Next door is where it's at. Try going into a different room and occupying yourself with something totally unrelated to music, leaving the track playing in your absence. Now listen to what needs doing.

- Smoothe the curve. The radio-friendly "pro" sound of most modern records, although not to everyone's taste, is nevertheless definitely familiar. This polished feel seems to rest in the mid EQ band, with producers tending to cut frequencies between 200Hz and 4kHz and cutting most in the 600Hz-1kHz region. On a graphic equaliser, EQing carried out like this forms a smooth, upside-down curve.

Professional producers often take down the mid range, as middle frequencies have a habit of tiring the ear and blocking the finer frequencies. This holds especially true with tracks that have a profusion of guitar. The "edge" that's apparently so desirable is achieved not by boosting the mid range, which seems natural, but by tweaking the top and bottom frequencies so that they interact with contrast.

OK, that's about it for EQ. Discovering how to use EQ properly is a steep learning curve, but experimentation and practice usually determine what's best for you.

remixing and sight – the visual take-over

"In theory, correctly synchronised sound and vision could be a tool for remixing human consciousness."
  Matt Black

magine if you will a small child, still too young to talk, locked in a *Clockwork Orange*-style cinema, strapped in with his or her eyes safely sticky-taped open. He's watching a random stream of images so mundane that they cross the threshold of disturbing. To stay in the present, the cinema is an Imax 360º surround-sound, vibration-equipped, 3D-feature hallucination machine. The child is bombarded with this overload of sight and sound, and yet he doesn't grow up to become Charles Manson or Elton John's flower arranger. You see, his brain has the ability to accommodate everything the cinema throws at him. He may not have the ability to understand the stream of images, but he can definitely process them. Every day, we suffer an incredibly vast intake of images, but aside from the occasional odd dream (which is 100 per cent remixing) we don't freak out or hide under the bedclothes – that is, unless this month's ketamine is particularly strong or you suffer from a very rare disorder known as synthesia.

There is a great deal of discussion about the information age and the MTV generation's obsession with visual stimulus. We are allegedly immersed in a constructed visual experience made up of hyper-real (ie not really real; more than real) images. Think of the TV you watch or the journey you make to the shops. You see people, buildings, rubbish, cars, food, trees, etc. In fact, if you tried to name every object you saw in a day, including those you saw on the television, you'd soon be knocking on the asylum door. What's remarkable is that these object are old, new, colourful, big, small, medium sized – in fact, any permutation you can think of will probably fit the character of an object viewed in an average day. The things you see are not related by any conventional links; they are totally random in their relationships. Amazingly, this bizarre onslaught is processed by our minds to become an orderly and sensible set of images. This nice linear processing lets us watch films and smile at the MTV animations.

Many sociologists and art critics argue that this mixing of old and new images that we experience in a normal day of work and watching TV damages internal narrative and personal aesthetic experience. They warn that, in essence, being bombarded by apparently unrelated images and harsh, mixed-up juxtapositions damages the psyche. On the other hand, this diversity of visual material that we see can be interpreted as a natural reflection of our minds. Our understanding is based in similes and comparisons. We think by splicing up experience into our own ideas and we retro-fit memories to beliefs. A dream is purely a series of images made up from all the sense memories we have collected over our entire lives. When you dream, your unconscious mind recycles imagery by using imagination, the most powerful editing suite in the universe. Dreams themselves are simply a more engrossed process of the communication between the conscious and unconscious mind that happens all the time. Sound familiar? A process whereby an original is altered to become something new? Yep, the same description applies to our old friend remixing. Of course, this doesn't mean that remixing – either visual or aural – is the physical embodiment of mind. After all, if all Descartes had needed to do was buy a Fatboy Slim single to illustrate the existence of consciousness, then…well, life truly would be a cruel joke.

The fact that remixing can act as a metaphor for mind simply shows that:

- any argument can be won with enough words. If people think remixing is a money-grabbing cop-out devoid of artistic merit, use long words to convince them otherwise;

- human behaviour is a reflection of human beings. In the same way that it's possible to determine where a stone fell in a puddle by the pattern of ripples, it's possible to find the presence of mind in any behaviour, especially creative exploits – ie remixing;

- remixing is a valid expression of an individual world view. Visual remixing, especially, often produces a result that's greater than the sum of its parts.

So we are visual creatures who have the ability to twist our surroundings and experiences into projects that exist outside ourselves. It seems that remixing is nothing new; it's been happening in our heads and on the streets for centuries. However, it's only recently that visual remixing has come into its own with programmes like *The Trip* and visual artists like Jorg Brightman. Visual remixing is a medium in itself. In fact, go and see a live dance act and they will invariable be playing against a backdrop of random imagery. The truest proponents of visual remixing onstage are probably Death In Vegas, but you could just as easily describe The Chemical Brothers' computer projections as visual recycling.

Just like its aural brother, visual remixing evolved through music, specifically dance music. The seeds for this reappropriation of imagery were sown with thousands of others in the run-up to the 1960s. For over 30 years, San Francisco has been the stomping ground of this art form. In the mid '60s, as the city was exploding into psychedelia, lightshows went hand in hand with acid tests. The images and patterns being projected onto the walls of legendary rock halls such as the Fillmore put vision to the movement spreading through the United States. Some bands would use old film projectors and splice together uncovered pieces of film into a random montage. Across the coast, The Velvet Underground with Andy Warhol and every amateur artist in New York were producing a darker kind of visual psychedelia. Warhol would edit random footage shot in the Warehouse, combining lights and oil lamps to create atmosphere, while the Warehouse's groupies would provide their own visual elements, using cameras and projectors to add to the confusion.

Of course, the idea of using film as a means of artistic expression beyond cinema was being explored much earlier than this. In 1957, Morrison Planetarium held a series of experimental artistic musical/visual events entitled the Vortex Project. Lighting systems and specially rigged projectors were installed along with a complex sound system, allowing artists to project images to the sounds of electronic and ethnic music. Slides and films were thrown onto the 60-foot-high dome along with star-machine projections while electronic music was woven through a huge sound system. In many ways, the Vortex Project foreshadowed the "superclubs" that we are now accustomed to. In fact, a very similar project was held at the Morrison Planetarium in 1992, with video projections shown on the dome to the recorded music of artists such as The Orb.

As San Francisco's beat movement paved the way for psychedelia, Elias Romero, a student of Seymore Lochs, was taking his projection ideas and using them within a new context. Romero would use liquid projections and film to create an environment for poets, dancers and other performers to work within. Together with Bill Ham, he is generally recognised as the true creator of the traditional San Francisco lightshow and, inadvertently, the godfather of visual remixing. Soon after this, all around the world artists began to combine sound and vision. In the UK, Pink Floyd's performances were heavily based on the lightshow. In fact, using normal imagery in unusual contexts with projections helped shape Pink Floyd's entire image.

In the early '90s, with the explosion of rave culture, parties in San Francisco such as Toontown, A Rave Called Sharon and the Gathering brought along a resurgence of visual remixing. The visuals here were not LA's bouncy-castle-style film loops being run over again and again on a wall all night, or Dr Seuss slide-projected onto a sheet; they were traditional psychedelic lightshows – large-scale, intricately composed collages of images constantly shifting into new forms and scenes. They progressed along with the music, rather than sitting beside it. This technique was being paralleled in fields all across the UK, but the visuals at that time weren't up to scratch with what was going on in San Francisco.

One thing that separated the new breed of lightshow from its predecessor of the '60s was the advent of new technological possibilities. At this time, computer capability was just beginning to reach the hands of artists. Graphics-manipulation programs were becoming readily available and thus a new world of visual possibilities opened. It was a world that allowed virtually anything you could imagine to be visually realised. This was the point at which visual remixing was transformed into something independent, spawning the "classic" (and very often dire) 3D landscapes and rotating shapes which seemed to star in the video of every dance record. However, it wasn't until The Future Sound Of London began to combine real and recognisable images with computer-generated landscapes that a more familiar form of visual remixing was born.

The sudden availability of equipment about which the '60s acid heads had only hallucinated meant that anyone with the inclination could remix images. A generation of kids who were brought up bombarded by MTV and television commercials were now able to fight back with their own visions of what their world was about – not Pepsi or Reebok but mind-expanding streams of images. (This is not to say that the majority of the MTV generation, Gen X or just plain young people were untickled by Reebok, only that a few computer owners actually produced something of note.)

Electronica has since embraced the new lightshow. There are clubs in which computer video systems are set up and the "VJ" artists come in with their software on disks, mixing them as if they were audio DJs. Coldcut have popularised the reinterpretation of images with their shows and software, and most budgeted electronic bands have their own visual counterparts who give vision to the music, for, as awesome as the music may be, it's not always that exciting to watch a couple of guys standing on a stage and twisting knobs on samplers.

So, simply, what *is* a visual remix? In his book *Expanded Cinema*, Gene Youngblood describes it as "a language that expresses not ideas, but a collective group consciousness". I prefer to view it as a process that directly mirrors its audio namesake, where an original piece – or, more often, a number of original pieces – is taken and reinterpreted to form a brand-new product.

"I like to think that the lightshow I'm doing is not simply guiding a visual experience but actually filtering through the bog of visual information and remixing it, redirecting it so that we are able to reinterpret and challenge what it is we can actually see."
Lon Clark, lightshow creator

but why?

"We are subverting visual space by creating 'acoustic space', a psychic and social environment that resembles the kind of space we perceive we hear: multi-dimensional, resonant, invisibly tactile, 'a total and simultaneous field of relations'."
Eric Davies (after McLuhan)

Music's correspondence with imagery actually stems much further back than the beat generation. Mozart could reputedly visualise his entire symphonies, not committing them to paper until the last moment. It's said that the act of writing was slower than the composer's imagination. Why labour over notation when the entire piece, timpani section and all, is available as quickly as a memory? Pythagoras saw parallels in all of the senses, viewing music and vision as the ultimate expression of understanding, while avant-garde composer Alexander Scriabin spent his life trying to combine music and colour to form a new musical notation.

The motives of creating synthesis are age old. Alchemy sees the Great Work as a total synthesis of sense and mind, body and soul, and visual remixing can be seen as an extension of this quest. To achieve a *gestalt* (whole) understanding, humans must combine elements with their concentric parts and view things from a distance. It's also innate human nature to find parallels in things. We are all dilettantes at heart, linking islands of information together with flimsy bridges. I see audio-visual remixing and the work of artists like Coldcut as an attempt to strengthen these bridges.

Is it not natural to combine clips with music? From the very first time that our ancestors watched the reflection of ripples on a cave wall and realised that the sound and appearance of the water were intricately linked, up to the most high-tech VJs, people have realised that it's all the same in the end. The wider the associations, the wider the understandings. The wider the understandings, the wider the enjoyment. What is music if not enjoyment of the senses? And remixing itself rests on the shoulders of association – or, rather, the expansion of association. When you combine familiarity (an original song) with something new (a remix), sense association expands. Mix that again with visual reinterpretation and you unearth a whole new set of possibilities.

On the other hand, visual remixing could be just clever eye-candy for body-fascist youths with too much TV experience. But still, eye-candy is ultimately fun.

The Trip – visual remixing comes home

Startled clubbers and undersexed night workers recently met confusion and joy while scanning through late-night TV. Nestling between *Freescreen* and *Open University*, they found a perplexing montage of images and music called *The Trip*. Jacques Peretti and DJ Downfall had created an audio-visual feast that combined footage from the public domain and NASA with home videos and leftfield electronica. Not quite chill-out music, not quite club visuals, *The Trip* is a synthesis that wanders happily into the field of audio-visual remixing. Jacques Peretti provides his own explanation.

JP: "Channel 4 asked me if I had any ideas for a late-night programme that would appeal to not just club people but tap into that post-club audience, intelligent as opposed to brainless, though I am quite a fan of brainless progs, even the chatback adverts which appear so fantastically between *The Trip*, which tell their own kind of truth. I suggested a programme that was as simple as it gets, just images to music and sounds, but not in a crap club-visuals way. The first series was quite clichéd in some respects, using NASA footage and so on, but over the last two series the programme has become increasingly strange and unconnected with the outside world – at least, so I hope. It has its own internal coherence and logic, and people who appreciate it are really, really, scarily into it. People who hate it simply think it's pretentious.

TP: "Will there be a new series?"

JP: "Yes. I want to use less of the esoteric footage from around the globe and more startling – and banal – footage of the present: CCTV footage; very domestic, low-key camcorder life – the camera tests and boring moments recorded at the beginnings and ends of tapes."

TP: "Is it visual remixing?"

JP: "Everything is visual remixing, really. There's no difference between *The Trip* and *Watchdog* with Anne Robinson. Sure, we take anything and find value in it, but we don't remix. *Auntie's Bloomers* is more of a remix in this respect, a [selection] of greatest hits cynically rehashed – a TV version of a Brandon Block mix album. We take images and treat them as if they were Etruscan fragments, pieces of the past given significance simply by being unearthed and shown to the public."

TP: "How did you choose the music and the clips, etc?"

JP: "The music is really just anything that works. We don't want to champion avant-hard music for its own sake, but we've found that we like a lot of its symphonic sweeps and weird textures. The programmes are very traditional in the sense that they have a beginning, a middle and an end, with all the obligatory dips and troughs of tone in between. The most memorable sound for me in the three series was simply a middle-aged man talking about his caravan holiday to Bridlington. It was freaky beyond anything overtly scary or self-consciously weird.

"In series two, we became very perverse and started to champion 'new dull' images – turbines, dead space on motorways, the unappealing subject matter of modern German photographers. We were keen on the static and tensely boring image as opposed to things that thought they were exciting. I don't think this worked as well as series three, by which time [we'd] honed the thing down to a fine art."

TP: "The trip could be compared to Burroughs' cut-up technique, allowing the viewer to piece together their own relevance and order. Is this intentional?"

JP: "Yes. They come together quite organically. There is a rigorous attention to creating a mood. It doesn't matter what images are used, really, as long as they intensify the mood."

TP: "You say that everything could be construed as remixing. Does the same go for club culture? How far removed in concept is Fabric to a college disco?"

JP: "Well, I'm not sure that clubs in themselves are as interesting as the social phenomena they illustrate [and] sometimes exemplify. A college disco and Fabric are identical, in the sense that [they] satisfy a well-defined market. The options for slippage – for social transgression – and the weird social collisions that make for a 'moment' probably wouldn't exist at either."

TP: "Post-modernism – a choking, bloated donkey wearing Fatboy Slim's mask or a valid philosophical stance nicely embodying dance music?"

JP: "Don't know what you're talking about. There are many, many theories regarding the texts of dance music, most discussed in that unintentionally hilarious and highly po-faced book *DJ Culture*. Dance music is just pop music, really. Derude have signature bleeps in each record, just like Buddy Holly chirruped so you'd know it was by him. What's the difference? What's amazing is not that people sample other people but that they don't do it more."

The Trip touches on ideas formulated by film-makers, most notably the work of Soviet Montage in the early 1900s, film-makers who, constricted by communism, created their art by fusing together imagery under heavy editing. It's said that Soviet Montage invented the idea of parallel time structures existing in one piece of film. Without Montage, the smooth story-telling of today's blockbusters would have never come into being. It's an interesting irony that early Montage film-makers made propaganda, and that much of *The Trip*'s iconography has its roots in propaganda.

Although shown on Channel 4 extremely late at night, *The Trip* has nevertheless managed to generate controversy, with Mr Peretti and DJ Downfall coming under serious fire, even though Channel 4 didn't screen certain scenes. Footage of lynchings and murders that were originally intended to be included were axed after complaints. Perhaps another parallel to Soviet Montage?

Comparisons are irrelevant, however, as the concept is one unto itself, and I'm sure Mr Peretti would hate mindless wandering. My personal favourite was the scene of a static, seated person, played to Gazza's version of 'Fog On The Tyne' cut to pieces and jumping on a bad CD player.

DIY audio-visual

practicalities

Audio-visual remixing is arguably the next step in music. Writing a new musical alphabet that exists on levels above sound can probably be considered the next major breakthrough in artistic expression, although universal association and the mapping of general images onto a musical stave are a long way off yet, and some would say that the idea is impossible. Nevertheless, the best music always conjures images, the best composers are still regarded as visionaries and, above all, audio-visual manipulation is fun, which is surely the key to all creativity.

Image-mashing and video-making used to be the pursuit of the rich and the process powered, but as the digital revolution (apologies for the hyperbole) is now under way some kind of tool or solution is available for all budgets. What follows is a brief run-down of the more popular and accessible programs.

VJamm

This is certainly the king of audio-visual remixing. Designed by Coldcut and CamArt, it places the musician firmly in control. As well as looking extremely well designed, its interface is accessible to even the most technophobic musician. Fully MIDI augmented, it allows you to load in your own video samples (as well as coming pre-equipped with 16 of its own), which you can then mix together at the touch of a button. Its controls allow DJ-like audio-scratching and numerous effects with pretty instantaneous response. As a live tool, it's light-years away from its competitors and it's extremely affordable. For more information, log onto www.ninjatune.net

PhotoJam

From Sony and Macromedia, the developers of Flash (the program that makes websites move), and principally designed as a web plug-in, PhotoJam nevertheless works as a free-standing interface. Basically, you create a folder of images and assign them to a piece of music. PhotoJam then reworks them in a series of set styles. The major drawback (aside from the static nature of the images) is the pre-ordained style of the reworking – the program only gives you presets to play with. In its favour, however, is its usability – anyone can instantly create PhotoJams. Download it free from the Flash website.

Director

Again developed by Macromedia, Director is the grandaddy of what we know as multimedia. Not immediately usable and slightly fiddly, relying heavily on scripting and light programming, it's primarily used for professional presentations. Definitely not the first choice for real-time remixing.

Finalcut Pro

The industry-favoured video-editing suite, developed by Apple. Pretty easy to use and a good interface, as you'd expect from Apple.

Adobe Premiere

The original desktop video-editing suite, which has improved since the halcyon days of Radius breakout boxes.

Hextatic and the clunk-click of audio-visual trips

There's no better illustration of the link between audio and visual samples than Hextatic, who came into being after the groundbreaking *Timber*, made in conjunction with Coldcut. Taking the idea of a one off "multisensory" work, Hextatic worked with sound and vision to create an entire album/film.

Rewind samples as readily from TV and visual culture as sound, computer games and kitchen implements. In its loosest sense, it's a re-conglomeration of culture references – Jimmy Saville dispenses travel advice while juxtaposed with electronica and Space Invaders samples. *Rewind* is not only the remixing of our surroundings but a reworking of the concept of an album. Bands had already experimented with mixed-mode CDs and putting videos on them as promos, but no one had created an album that was totally dual sensory.

TP: "Firstly can you give us a bit of background on Hextatic?"

ROBIN BRUNSON: "I met Stuart [Warren-Hill] at a Channel 5 launch party, and he mentioned that they needed someone to do some 3D animation where he was working. I'd recently finished a post-grad in Computer Imaging and was bored with the corporate work I was doing and so decided to go and talk to Stu about possibly doing some stuff. When I officially went to meet him, I found that he was working for Hex Media [alias Coldcut and Rob Pepperell], which was quite a surprise as Coldcut had been musical heroes of mine. Stuart was working on *Timber* and I basically started doing animation stuff for Coldcut's *Let Us Play* album. I ended up doing the 3D characters of Coldcut that featured on the album artwork, and Stuart and I then worked together on the video for 'Beats And Pieces'. And that's how it all started."

TP: "Tell us a bit about *Rewind*."

RB: "The idea just stemmed from *Timber* really. Once Stuart had finished touring with Coldcut, he had the idea of carrying on from where *Timber* left off and doing a whole audio-visual album. I was really keen to get involved, and we found we had similar tastes in music and retro culture. We were both really into old-school arcade games and early electro music, so it seemed natural. The first track we made was 'Vector', which encompassed all this, and it basically spiralled from there. We wanted to put all those misspent days down the arcade to some sort of use! Copyright-wise, we're usually pretty careful. There's a whole world of untapped stuff out there, like there was when people first started sampling audio, really obvious things, like the Jimmy Saville sample we got cleared. We're a small act on a reasonably small label, so it's that kind of philosophy where, if you're not making any money from it, it's not really worth chasing you."

TP: "On *Rewind*, which came first, audio or visual clips?"

RB: "Usually, it's about coming up with a theme beforehand and then going away, finding or creating the source material, sampling it all off and making the tracks. We'll then edit it, but it usually gets turned around in the editing stage and we'll change it there, then go back, etc. It changes every time. Some of the tracks – like 'Deadly Media' – were done purely in video-editing programs and used no music sequencing at all. It's pretty intense, doing it that way, but in a sense it's the purest expression of what we do."

TP: "Do you think there's any direct correspondence between sound and vision? If so, can sound exist as maps of colour and picture?"

RB: "Well, naturally, if you think about it. Yeah, we think it's the way forward for music in general. With DVD getting more popular, it will hardly be worth just listening to music alone. I think some artists have already experimented mapping sound to colour, etc. I think our stuff will probably get more abstract in future, but at the moment it's more about straight-up visual reference."

TP: "Marshall McLuhan talks about the visual space invading the auditory stream. Do you think that what you and projects like *The Trip* do is the opposite?"

RB: "I think our live shows probably translate that exactly."

TP: "Tell us a bit about the Big Chill events."

RB: "Stuart's been involved since the start, doing slides and projections early on and then moving into video. They've always supported our stuff 100 per cent, and last year's show at the Enchanted Garden was the culmination of two years' work and probably the highlight of our careers so far. Thousands of fans outdoors in one of the most beautiful settings in England. What more can you say."

TP: "Can comparisons be drawn to what you do and the work of early lightshow artists and acid tests?"

RB: "Kind of, I think. I think what we do is more literal – people tend to concentrate on the screens and be entertained by that mix of audio and visual, as opposed to just creating an 'environment'."

TP: "Is the future of music a synthesis with other media, like *Rewind* being a CD-ROM? Do you think other artists will start to exploit technology as a medium equal to music?"

RB: "Like I said earlier about DVD, I think it's inevitable."

TP: "Does visual remixing exist?"

RB: "Yes. With *Timber* we also did it, getting people like EBN [the Emergency Broadcast Network] and Lucky People Center to do audio-visual remixes. It was great, because they were a big influence on us."

TP: "Do you think VJs should get higher billing, *à la* the old lightshows at the Fillmore, where Jimi Hendrix shared billing with the lightshow artist?"

RB: "It's getting better. Ninja have always billed their VJs equally, and it seems to be happening a bit more in the more forward-thinking clubs."

TP: "What are your views on straight audio remixing?"

RB: "I'm not against it. I've done a few myself."

TP: "Is it valid as a form of music or does it simply exploit listeners by rehashing old tunes?"

RB: "I think it's great for DJs, which is where it came from. Plus, in a way, you get extra content that wasn't there a few years ago."

TP: "Where does an original begin and a remix end?"

RB: "Some remixes bear no resemblance to the original at all, which can either annoy or delight. Personally, I'm really into dodgy bootlegs that fuse lots of really good tracks together. They always work extremely well in clubs."

TP: "Is it safe to say – as expressed by Jacques Peretti – that, in essence, all visual media is a form of remixing?"

RB: "Maybe, but there's a lot of stuff out there that is completely new, I think, more so than music, which even in its purest form can always be seen as a rehash of something, I think."

TP: "You sample a great deal from your surroundings by re-contextualising the everyday. Is it possible to change perception? Even to go as far as remixing consciousness, as expressed by Matt Black?"

RB: "Yes, definitely. I think *Timber* did that in a way, ie putting a really strong message forward. I think our stuff is a bit more about nostalgia, which is also really powerful in capturing your audience."

TP: "Could the re-contextualisation of everyday sounds and pictures possibly lead to a greater understanding of our surroundings?"

RB: "Yes. Some people say music does this already, but I think audio-visual is a more [valid] medium."

TP: "Lon Clark, a lightshow creator, sees visual remixing as a knife that can cut through the bog of information we are bombarded with on a daily basis. Fair?"

RB: "Yes. It's a great tool for cutting out all the crap and re-presenting what you think is really important."

TP: "What plans do you have in the future?"

RB: "To expand the live show and get into DVD production and DVDJing. Remix your life. It's fun!"

Coldcut and reality manipulation

"The world is God's imperfect sketch. It is the job of the artist to reinterpret it in his own vision."
   Vincent Van Gogh

There is an old Discordian saying that's whispered from priest to priest. Unfortunately, no one knows what it is. In an attempt to remedy this, I heard a rumour that Malkuth the Younger pried random pieces of the world together whenever asked to recite the saying. If he was beside a swimming pool, the quote would read, "Never swim, lest he who cannot grows cold."

Likewise, if asked beside a school, the phrase would become, "Learn – a building is not a word."

Versatility and adaptation are the heart of any understanding and very much a trait of Zen masters Coldcut, the pioneers of cut-up and reinterpretation. They began life in 1987, and their debut single, 'Say, Kids (What Time Is It)?', was the first sample-built record in the UK. Constantly changing form and approach, Coldcut played ball with major labels before breaking away and creating Ninja Tune, their own label, in 1993. "Mix hippie ideals with a certain amount of sound business practice," as they say, and you have one of the most artistically valid labels in existence.

Coldcut consists of Matt Black and ex-art teacher Jonathan More. Aside from developing VJamm, Coldcut are luminaries in remix circles for their reworking of Eric B And Rakim's 'Paid In Full', which some say defined the word *remix*. Their own work, as well as their label's output, goes from strength to strength, but we're concerned here with the aspect of art that they've touched on with VJamm.

VJamm is an extension of DJing, going beyond sound to allow real-time manipulation of video, and Coldcut are edging towards finally capturing Pythagoras' music of the spheres, the sound of our universe. As Matt Black explains here, technology is slowly enabling us to reinterpret the world – not in a static way but in real time, a constantly evolving stream. To reinterpret is to see more clearly and have fun. The artist always knows his medium, and Coldcut see life as their preferred medium, mutating sound, vision and thought in an ultimate remix.

If all of their goals are achieved, it will be full-sense, immersive-reality remixing. The music of the spheres implied cosmic fusion, the assumption that the universe embodies a divine geometrical harmony, whereas this harmony is mirrored in all natural phenomena, both in microcosm and macrocosm. The harmonies of celestial orbits parallel the seeming irregularities of life-forms on Earth. The bases of these correspondences are mathematically precise vibrations manifested as light, sound, smell and other sensory stimuli. Fusing perceptions of these seemingly discrete sensory inputs is synaesthesia, which Pythagoras considered the greatest philosophical gift and spiritual achievement. Coldcut's aims run alongside this Pythagorean philosophy, and VJamm is the first step toward expanding human consciousness beyond music.

Things, as always, are clear when explained by their creators. The following interview with Matt Black will hopefully illuminate not only VJamm but also the concept of remixing as a whole.

TP: "Firstly, could you tell us a little bit about your involvement in VJamm?"

MB: "VJamm was developed by Coldcut in conjunction with Cambridge Arts – CamArt – who programmed it for us. I heard that EBN, the Emergency Broadcast Network, had a MIDI-controlled video-sample player, and I wanted one, so we thought we'd make our own. We met Cambridge Arts at the Big Chill. CamArt had already been working along those lines and Coldcut had done some art installations. We wanted to have an instrument that allowed us to jam with audio-visual samples in the same way we'd been able to jam with audio samples, which is how Coldcut had been making a living for the last 14 years or so."

TP: "You were a programmer yourself?"

MB: "My first proper job was with Logica and I used to program early graphics systems for them. I don't know if I was a very good programmer, but it was interesting. I've always been into the idea of computers, particularly the creative uses of them. I remember when we started Coldcut, in 1987, we started to get a bit of money and I went out and bought an Amiga with a frame-grabber and Deluxe Paint and stuff. It was just brilliant to be able to directly manipulate images on the screen. To unify this visual manipulation with sound was a natural goal, really."

TP: "How has VJamm developed since the initial version?"

MB: "We've been using VJamm for the live show for over three years now. The initial version allowed playback of video samples at the touch of a key. There's [also] a pro version available. Our goal is to make these tools as widely available as possible. Were not really looking to do a Bill Gates on it; keeping it exclusively for ourselves, for our own art, is not what we set out to do. The whole point is to [develop] interest in this field, and the best way to do that is let as many people have it as possible... It's too good to keep [for] ourselves. So there are three versions available – a free version with Coldcut's *Let Us Play*, a cheap version at £30 and a pro version [for] £200 to £300, both available from the Ninja website.

"The main difference between the pro and the cheaper version is that you can use it full-screen. But when you compare it to other professional video software, at £1,000-plus, it's very reasonably priced. With the pro version, you also get the developers' kit of VJamm 2."

TP: "Can you tell us about version two?"

MB: "VJamm 2 is a huge expansion of what you can do. VJamm is a relatively simple program in comparison, though people who have seen it have been gobsmacked by it. I've shown it to people like Jean-Jacques Perrey and Carl Craig, and they've been absolutely fascinated by it, which is very gratifying. VJamm 1 was based on the scratch-DJ paradigms – ie one hand scratches one record as the other hand moves the crossfader. For our live shows, we actually bolted an extra crossfader onto our audio mixer for this purpose. The second crossfader controls a video-mixer crossfade – quite crude, but very effective.

"VJamm 2 moves away from this monophonic scratch-DJ paradigm, giving what you'd call polyphony if it was a synthesiser. VJamm 2 gives you the ability to play up to 16 clips simultaneously onscreen. They can be sized and positioned any way you want, like a virtual video wall where you can change and move the monitors around. In the second version, we've brought in a whole load of new functions and put them all under MIDI control – zoom, stretch, positioning [and] lumakey have all been given MIDI control. The pitch bend will actually pitch the sound while slowing down or speeding up the video clip."

TP: "When can we see the new version?"

MB: "A lot of the new functions will be showcased in a new Coldcut project called *Cooking With Coldcut*. We've taken lots of audio-visual samples of a kitchen and put them in a *Timber*-style piece, except having more than one clip onscreen at a time increases the intensity somewhat."

TP: "You've spoken before about hypertext and the potential of technology expanding thought as well as music."

MB: "It is a new art form, a new kind of instrument. I'm not saying we're the masters of a new art form, because we're just toddling around in the playground. What we *are* doing is saying [that] the playground is open. And I'm absolutely confident that people will, you know, come in and play.

"Multimedia is a somewhat over-used term. Synaesthesia is a somewhat over-used term. I'd go back to someone like Scriabin, who said he planned his masterpiece as a liturgical enactment in which scent, coloured light, poetry, singing and music would unite to produce a final, supreme ecstasy. So, in theory, correctly synchronised sound and vision could be a tool for remixing human consciousness."

TP: "Slightly similar to Throbbing Gristle's idea? [Throbbing Gristle had a theory, inherited from alchemy, that a certain combination of notes played at the right time with the correct atmosphere could produce altered states up to and beyond enlightenment.]"

MB: "Yes, and I have a great deal of respect for Throbbing Gristle and bands like Coil. What's different now is that we have the technology, so a much larger number of people can afford access to these toys and tools, which should hopefully increase the diversity of ideas and the amount of material which will feed into it.

"One thing I would say about Throbbing Gristle and Coil is that I'm very much into light. [TG had very overt ties with chaos magic and Thelema, and the epic noise jams favoured by the group could hardly be construed as fun.] I agree with a Buddhist poet [Thich Nhat Han] who said that art should reveal and heal. I think it's quite easy to reveal with art, especially the darker side of things, but to heal... That's perhaps a bit more challenging."

TP: "I actually read somewhere that doctors were using certain frequencies to treat illnesses."

MB: "Yes, including the study of cymatics, invented by Doctor Hans Jenny. This includes the use of sound to treat medical conditions. Without getting overly cosmic, we do consist of vibrations. We are made up of matter. Matter is energy. Energy vibrates. The wave/particle duality nicely illustrates this. So here we are, all resonating away. It surely seems natural that all these resonances interact, interfere and harmonise with each other. There's something fundamental with music that ties in with that. Humans like music because it can act as a kind of interface with the cosmos."

TP: "It's interesting that you see music as a kind of frequency translator for the universe and are involved with VJamm, because sight essentially operates in frequencies as well – much finer frequencies, but still frequencies."

MB: "Yeah. Living organisms are extremely sensitive to energy, because that's what we are. Anyway, we're probably getting slightly off the subject."

TP: "Is visual remixing a valid term for what you and projects like *The Trip* are doing?"

MB: "Well, yes, it's really audio-visual remixing. In the earlier days of what we were doing, we'd go along to where a DJ was playing and we'd mix visuals along with what they were doing. The human would provide the kind of interface to it and select the material that was appropriate as best they could. Before that, when I was at school, I had a sound-to-light generator, which would just flash the lights in time with the music. The whole point of VJamm is to make the connection between sound and vision absolutely fundamental. Sound and vision are linked – it's basic. We live in an audio-visual reality. I've got a wicked quote on a tape about cymatics, which I used on an album: 'Everything owes its existence to sound.' You know, 'In the beginning was the word,' etc, and with vision, *fiat lux* – let there be light – you have an audio-visual species wrapped in an audio-visual experience. Sound and light – vision – are two aspects of the same thing. [Feel free, dear reader, to draw a comparison here with the particle/wave duality.] Coming from a DJ background and then mixing visuals with what I DJ'd, the next step was to synchronise the two, possibly a new thing altogether.

"I'd love to be able to bring smell-o-vision into the whole thing as well. The connection between smell and memory would be great to add. And, of course, touch and any other senses you care to mention, especially a sense of humour. What Coldcut and VJamm do is possibly closer to *musique concrète* than visual remixing. That and photo-collage."

MB: "Except using far more advanced technology."

TP: "Yes. But it all feeds into the same thing. All types of information can be digitised and manipulated. That's really what we're doing."

MB: "Where, in your opinion, does remixing end and originality begin?"

TP: "Well, it's a spectrum, like most things. At one end, if you take a single drumbeat and make a new track that uses that drumbeat, you can fairly safely claim you are making an original. At the other end you'd be sampling a complete Beatles chorus and sticking a drum loop underneath it. Call that an original and you will be hearing from The Beatles' lawyers. And it's fair that you should do, because you're stealing a large slice. But then, maybe music is a joyful sound to be created and shouldn't be copyrighted at all. I suggest, however, that you're not doing anything that clever if you take huge bits.

"In the middle of the spectrum is the territory where we're really all operating. With VJamm, if you look at the samples that come with it, there's stuff we've nicked from the TV we think we can get away with, there's public-domain footage or there's NASA footage that's all public domain, an incredible resource. I think a lot more footage should be public domain, really. I mean, anything the BBC do should be public domain. We pay the licence fee for it all to be shot so we should be able to mutate it if we want."

TP: "The idea of visual possession or copyright is much, much harder to define than audio."

MB: "Yes. The legal field for music copyright infringement is quite well defined."

TP: "It's like views. If someone looks at a mountain, do they own the view?"

MB: "Well, someone could take a photo of it and say, 'This is mine.' Then someone else could go to exactly the same place and take an identical photo, turn around and say, 'Well, actually, it's mine.' Those sorts of things are very difficult to assign an ownership status. I guess it's all generalities; I don't think there's a particular right or wrong. You just look at what you're doing and say, 'Am I doing this out of love? Am I putting in creative input of my own or am I just reappropriating someone else's work to make a lot of money?'

"You can usually tell by people's work and what they do with the money they make out of it. A kid can sample *Terminator* and Walt Disney and make a mix on his desktop which entertains him and his kid brother. Why shouldn't they do that? It's his rental fees that pay Walt Disney's dividends. If you want to release that, put it on MTV and get paid for it, it will be a totally different scenario."

TP: "Have you run into any copyright difficulties?"

MB: "It's difficult, sometimes, dealing with the big companies. It's not that they're evil, so much – though they can be – it's that they're stupid. So, so stupid. Like with Disney. We used 'I'm The King Of The Swingers', from *The Jungle Book*, and Disney would like us to stop using that."

TP: "Because obviously your song will damage the sales of *The Jungle Book*."

MB: "Exactly. See, you know what I mean. They didn't say, 'Guys, we really like what you're doing. Why don't we talk about doing a remix of

The Jungle Book so everybody gets sorted?' They're asleep, unfortunately. And the lawyers have too much motivation for keeping suing people."

TP: "Any closing thoughts?"

MB: "Um… I think that art is something fundamental to human existence, and I think art is about Man's groping attempts to touch the divine, and that motivation is where real art comes from. And I think that is the Great Work, to continue that tradition, the search for Man's evolution. It's either that or be wiped out by machines, *Terminator* style. I think eventually we will develop artificial consciousness and artificial life-forms which, a lot of the time, will be able to do things much better than us. I have a suspicion that our own evolution will involve a fusion between Man and machine consciousness. Unless we can keep up our own evolution, there's not much really for us to hang around for."

outro

The world is flat.

It's true. The first space tourist sent me an email to prove it. What's that got to do with remixing? Nothing, as such, only that you shouldn't believe everything you read.

A friend of mine once told me about a sage (yes, another one) who explained life in terms of "notnormal" and "not normal". As long as everything was "notnormal", life was going just fine. But if you ever found yourself behaving in a "not normal" way (stress on the normal) then trouble was brewing.

Music is born from deviation. Art is born from twisting the medium into something new. So why not use remixing as a tool to twist your style? Taking someone else's song and changing it about just isn't normal. It's notnormal.

Another of this sage's comments was to do with ants being the font of quantum causality: "Our aim in life may well be to step on one single ant, and our destiny is fulfilled when we have performed that task. How will we know our job is done? Well, we will be the ant." I like that. Sometimes you have to step on yourself to reach enlightenment. Amongst cake and scurrying confusion, God's Nikes crush you and *boom* – destiny fulfilled. No reason. Just that.

Consider that when trying to fit a 60bpm vocal to a trance bass line. What's the solution? Crush the vocal line into something entirely new. If you stamp on it hard enough, I'm sure it will eventually fit.

websites

hat follows are some of the better websites linked to remixing. The Internet is a surprising desert when it comes to websites dealing with the practical side of remixing. That said, however, there is a wealth of samples, production information and interviews that can be applied.

general

www.ninjatune.net (superb site and home to great music)
www.g-stoned.com (for all your dub needs)
www.timespace.com (the ultimate sample supplier for the UK)
www.progression.co.uk
www.hyperreal.com
www.audiovisualizers.com
www.volumeone.com
www.bigchill.net
www.one9ine.com/
www.artistica.org/
www.adbusters.org/
www.atrecordings.com
www.musiques-electroniques.com
www.rocketnetwork.com
www.intermusic.com
www.emulation.net
www.moviesounds.com/
www.disinfo.net (ultimate knowledge source)
www.warprecords.com
www.djdownfall.co.uk/
www.cybersales.co.uk/music/indie/abuse
www.chachacha.co.uk/uninf/
www.utopiadjs.com/remixing.html

www.universaltribe.com/remixing.html (streaming site that allows uploads of your work)

www.arktikos.com/bjork/ (fan remix site devoted to the reworkings of Björk)

www.grandroyal.com/remix/ (remix The Beastie Boys)

www.loopers-delight.com

www.rawilson.com

MIDI file sites

www.prs.net (huge archive of classical MIDI files)

www.newtronic.com (list of dance-orientated MIDI programming and software)

www.themidicity.com

www.midifarm.com

visual remixing sites

This is a kind of grey area that spills into film and sociology, although it's guaranteed interesting reading. These are the best resources.

www.camart.co.uk/vjpro/

www.ninjatune.net/coldcut/disco/lup/htpr/ (hypertext of Coldplay's *Let Us Play*)

www.urbanvisuals.com

www.toneburst.com

www.imaja.com

www.cinetrip.net

www.4later.com/trip.html (check out *The Trip* here)

www.quicktime.com

www.mentalwaste.8m.com/remixes.html

software sites

www.rhime.com/

www.d-lusion.com/products/mj/index.html

www.mixman.com

www.crmav.com/dictionary/remixing.shtml

www.interphase.be/redsound.html

www.ss7x7.com/

www.groovemaker.com/

www.dspstudio.de/

www.sonicfoundry.com/

sequencing software

www.steinberg.de
www.emagic.de
www.cakewalk.com
www.opcode.com

company homepages

Yamaha
www.yamaha.com

Roland
www.rolandcorp.com

Korg
www.korg.com

Akai
www.akai.com/akaipro/index.html

Novation
www.nova-uk.com

Ninja Tune
www.ninjatune.net

other labels worth looking at

American Bacon Recordings
www.americanbacon.com

Asphodel
www.asphodel.com

Astralwerks
www.caroline.com/astralwerks

Blue Note
www.bluenote.com

Bungalow Records
www.bungalow.de

Clean Up
www.cleanup.music.co.uk

Dorado Records
www.dorado.net/

Compost Records
www.compost-records.com/

ECM Records
ecm.com

The Fez (Italy)
www.mediatec.it/fez

Fi-Sci Records
www.fisci.freeserve.co.uk

The Beastie Boys
www.grandroyal.com/

Hospital Records
www.hospitalrecords.com

Hefner/Victor Malloy
www.inertia.co.uk/

Metalheadz
www.metalheadz.co.uk

Mo'Wax
www.mowax.com

Planet E
www.planet-e.net

Mush (birthplace of cLOUDDEAD)
www.dirtyloop.com

Pork Recordings (Fila Brazillia)
www.pork.co.uk/

Pussyfoot

www.pussyfoot.co.uk

R&S Records
www.rsrecords.com

Rawkus
www.rawkus.com

Renegade Records
www.tovmusic.com

Strata-East Records (jazz label)
www.serecs.com

Studio !K7
www.studio-k7.de/

Talkin' Loud
www.talkinloud.com/

Ubiquity Records
www.ubiquityrecords.com

Underground Resistance
www.undergroundresistance.com/

un-easy listening

This may well be a case of pointing out the obvious, but in order to gain a good grounding in remixing a knowledge of good remixes is quite important. What follows is a very brief list of what I consider to be remixes worth listening to. At best it will serve as a discography for the book. Of course, there are too many to mention.

- *The K&D Sessions* – Kruder And Dorfmeister. Seminal double album with classic mixes of Depeche Mode, Bomb The Bass and Lamb. The Viennese twins of dub surface on every chill-out compilation you care to mention. Remix and additional production by Hybrid, with nu-skool breaks aplenty as they remix BT, Andreas Jonson, the all-powerful 'Papua New Guinea' by FSOL and Moby.

- 'Don't Die Just Yet' – David Holmes. An EP-length single which heavily samples Serge Gainsbourg. Unusually remixed by Dakota and The Chemical Underground Crew, Mogwai and Arab Strap. Holmes himself also offers a take.

- *Bletch* – various. A kind of "best of" from Warp Records, mixed and remixed by DJ Food.

- 'Brown Paper Bag' – Roni Size. Pretty lame music for the buying of flatpack furniture, enlivened by Photek's superb, bass-heavy cut.

- *Cargo Remixes* – Sofa Surfers. Remix album from the Viennese dub outfit.

- *An Electric Storm* – White Noise. Tired of arguing over Can's and Kraftwerk's lineage to electronica? If so, then check out this 1960s slice of electronica, which is as fresh as Leaf's unreleased thought processes.

- _Papercut_ – Faultline. EP with a superlative remix of Faultline's superlative aural construction 'Mute'.

- _Cold Krush Cuts_ – DJ Food, Coldcut and DJ Krush. Remixes and versions in this Ninja Tune double-mix album.

- _Tone Tales From Tomorrow Too_ – various. Coldcut take a remixed ride around the Ntone catalogue.

- _Remixes By…_ – The Cinematic Orchestra. Incredible and inspiring reworkings of some lesser-known tracks.

- _Motion_ – The Cinematic Orchestra.

- _Suzuki In Dub_ – Tosca. Some pleasantly upbeat remixes of Dorfmeister's dubby _Suzuki_.

- _Solid Ether_ – Nils Petter Molvær. ECM-signed trumpeter takes on dance with jazz perfection.

legal issues, stretching terms and specifications

how to save memory

Although not quite the issue it was five years ago, sampler memory is still a problem. The irritation of not having enough room for the last cymbal lick is beyond words, so here are some basic tips that will hopefully help you to avoid premature baldness.

• At a full audio bandwidth of 20kHz, using a 44.1kHz sampling rate, one minute of stereo sound takes up around 10MB of RAM. If you can make do with mono samples, this immediately doubles the amount of sampling time available.

• If you can tolerate a lower audio bandwidth, setting a lower sampling rate can extend your sampling time by a factor of two or more.

• When sampling sustained musical sounds such as strings or flutes, another time-saving strategy is looping the sample (not to be confused with sampling the loop, which I'll come onto later). Most sustained sounds have a distinctive attack portion, but then, as they start to decay, the sound becomes more consistent. Listen to something like a flute or a string section playing a sustained note and you'll notice that very little about the sound changes after the initial attack. This being the case, there's no reason to sample the whole sound being played. Simply sample the first few seconds and then use your sampler's editing facilities to create a loop so that the middle part of the sample repeats itself continually until you release the key. Obviously, there's little point in trying to loop short or percussive sounds – they probably wouldn't sound right, anyway – but you can loop long percussive sounds, such as the decay of a cymbal.

NB: There's another good reason for looping sounds, and that's to get around the fact that the length of a sample changes as you play higher or lower on the keyboard. And besides, the length of this original sound will probably be too short if you want to hold down a string pad for the next 24 bars. Once a sound is looped, its level never has to decay to zero, because the same section of sound is being continuously looped.

• The use of panning can be an effective way of fooling listeners into believing that they're inhabiting a stereo world in your memory-dictated mono realm. The most obvious and straightforward panning arrangement for a mono multisample is to pan sounds to one side at the bottom of the keyboard and then to pan things through the centre and to the opposite side as you progressively play higher up the keyboard. (Some samplers have this panning "template" as an onboard option.) Simply panning sounds alternately left and right will give you an effective stereo image, and the apparent size of your multisampled instrument(s) will be doubled. However, if you're willing to venture under your sampler's bonnet and get your hands dirty, there are a number of multisample panning tricks that can open up new stereo-soundscape possibilities to you. Here is a set of maps.

	NARROW	WIDE
Low	L05/R05	L10/R10
	L10/R10	L20/R20
	L15/R15	L30/R30
	L20/R20	L40/R40
High	L25/R25	L50/R50

	STAGGERED	STEREO POSITIONAL (L/R)
Low	L05/R10	L50/R10
	L15/R20	L40/R20
	L25/R30	L30/R30
	L35/R40	L20/R40
High	L45/R50	L10/R50

"Narrow" and "wide" stereo-panning patches can also be layered on top of one another and switched between, via velocity switching or crossfading, which widens the stereo image the harder you play. Here are some rough outlines, but take into account your personal playing style for the velocity rates.

VELOCITY SWITCH	VELOCITY CROSSFADE	PANNING
0-90	0-110	L05/R05 (soft)
91-127	80-127	L10/R10 (loud)
0-90	0-110	L10/R10 (soft)
91-127	80-127	L20/R20 (loud)
0-90	0-110	L15/R15 (soft)
91-127	80-127	L30/R20 (loud)
0-90	0-110	L20/R20 (soft)
91-127	80-127	L40/R40 (loud)
0-90	0-110	L25/R25 (soft)
91-127	80-127	L50/R50 (loud)

sample CDs

Sample CDs are a confusing phenomenon to the traditional musician stumbling into the realm of music technology, not so much in application but rather in concept. The idea of using ready-made riffs and drum loops as a basis for "original" music has had many of my classically trained friends scratching their heads. Needless to say, working with some construction-based loop CDs has a lot in common with remixing. In fact, if you wish to practise remixing alien material, investing in a song-based sample CD isn't the worst thing you can do.

The concept of copyright and sample CDs is also strange. Most offer the user licence but not ownership of the samples. This means that you can use them in commercial projects but not sell them or distribute them in sample form. They come in a variety of formats, colours and concepts. Here's a brief overview.

audio CDs

Pros

- They're cheap.
- There's a large number of available releases.
- They offer the quick and easy auditioning of sounds.
- They're compatible with every possible sampling format.

Cons

- It can be very time consuming and fiddly to sample and store large numbers of sounds.
- You need a good knowledge of your sampler's workings to get the most from an audio sample CD.

CD-ROMs

Pros

- With these, it's quick and easy access to all sounds.
- You need to spend less time sampling.
- You can give your songs an instantly "professional" touch.
- They often contain more sounds than audio CDs.

Cons

- They're more expensive, sometimes incredibly so.
- You have no chance to audition sounds without loading them (although this depends on the format).
- They don't always encourage the user to experiment as much as they could.

mixed-mode CDs

Pros

- These are often the same price as audio CDs, and sometimes even cheaper.
- They can offer the best of both worlds, both audio and ROM data.
- They're good for auditioning sounds on a regular CD player before loading up samples.

Cons

- Having to fit both file types on a single disc can mean less samples.
- Although nearly all popular sampler formats can be catered for on a mixed-mode release, WAV and AIFF are the most common these days, which isn't to everyone's tastes.

Sample CDs are available from places like Time & Space in the UK (www.timespace.com) or other similar shops.

Coldcut comments

The May 2000 edition of the Australian *Zebra* magazine interviews Coldcut on the subject of sampling.

ZM: "What are your feelings about the use of sampling in the production of music?"

CC: "Sampling is now a very widely used tool in the production of music. In fact, there is probably not a record in the charts in any country today which doesn't use sampling in some way, hence its use in music production appears to be legitimised, even though there was considerable opposition to it when the technique was first introduced. If one agrees that sampling is a tool in music production, all tools are legitimate – a hammer can be used to smash someone's skull or build a house – so it's the *use* of a tool that is crucial, and it's the use of samples which sometimes raises questions about the originality of the samplers and their compositions."

ZM: "In contemporary music, do you think that sampling is building upon existing ideas?"

CC: "It depends entirely how the sampling is used. For instance, I can go into the supermarket and sample the ambience of clashing trolleys and people arguing and make that into a piece, so I'm not using anyone else's ideas, other than the ambience of the public, which is available to an artist to use. I don't think sampling is essential to what contemporary music really is. Sampling really is no different to recording, [and the] recording of music has been in existence for 100 years or so and has become extremely popular, but it is not essential to music; it is merely widely used."

ZM: "Who do you think uses a sampler effectively?"

CC: "As I said, the history of sampling goes back a long way, and I think the *musique concrète* pioneers like John Cage, Pierre Henri and Jean-Jacques Perrey use the technique very effectively. Particularly I've found impressive Jacques Perrey's use of short percussive samples, sequenced together with immense effort involved in cutting and splicing tapes with that degree of precision, before [the] convenience of the sampler was available. I find that work very inspiring. Double Dee And Steinski, before the use of digital samplers, used multitrack tape to collage sounds together – [that] was amazing. And sound collage is actually what we're talking about, rather than sampling. On the other extreme, many rich artists were able to afford samplers before they became cheaper; something like the Synclavier 20, years ago, probably cost £200,000, and only rich artists who usually made rather boring work could afford them."

samples, copyright and the law

Copyright is a horribly entangled issue. Every musician has a different opinion about it, while the law tends to stick to one. As with anything legal, copyright law has an unhealthy fascination with semantics. Reams and reams of documentation deal with the subject, but some basic points are worth noting.

There are three owners of the copyright in a sample:

- The publisher of the original piece of music;
- The record company (or film company, if the sample is from a film or video) who released it and therefore own the performance of the music or speech;
- The owner of the moral rights to the copyright (which, for a piece of music, lie ultimately with the original composer).

These days, most music-related contracts have a clause which states that the composer waives the moral rights to their work. Having said that, there are two issues on which a composer – or the custodian of his copyright – can insist. One is the right of *paternity*, which means that he can insist on being fully credited in the songwriting credits. The other is the right of *integrity*, a precept as familiar to remixers as picket fences are to Klan members. Integrity means that, if an artist doesn't like the new track that uses his material, for whatever reason, he can block the use of his work. In fact, if any of the three owners of the copyright refuse permission for you to use their property, there's nothing you can do about it; two out of three isn't enough.

how are copyright issues resolved?

These are the main types of deal you can strike with companies.

A Buy-Out Fee

This is a one-off payment for the use of the sample. Breakbeat CDs work on this principle.

A Percentage Deal

There are two ways in which this kind of deal works:

- The owner of the sample will become co-owner of your track and will be paid royalties directly;

- You will pay the owner of the sample an agreed royalty rate on every copy of your material that's pressed.

The difference between the two is that, in the second case, you will still own the copyright to your track, as opposed to owning only a percentage of it. This is known officially as *financial participation*.

A Roll-Over Fee

With this kind of agreement, you pay an agreed amount of money for the number of records pressed. This saves having to calculate royalty payments. Everything is open to negotiation, including whether you need to credit the source of your sample (which is usually required). Of course, you may be able to come to some other arrangement that is agreeable to all sides – sample clearance is still in its infancy. Whatever deal you strike, get it in writing and stick to your side of the bargain.

other information

For further information on the subject of sampling copyright, contact the MCPS's Sample Clearance Department at the address below:

Mechanical Copyright Protection Society Limited
Sample Clearance Department
Elgar House
41 Streatham High Road
London SW16 1ER

Tel: +44 (0)20 8769 7702
Fax: +44 (0)20 8664 4698

(The MCPS's main switchboard number is +44 (0)20 8664 4400, for all enquiries not to do with sample clearance.)

Thanks to *Sound On Sound* magazine for the information provided here.

glossary

T his is the longest section of this entire book, a glossary of terms for the curious, confused and anally retentive. Aside from pure reference, those of you who still haven't found a name for your band will find amusing suggestions in some definitions. (Aphex isn't Greek, you see.)

absorption

Short for the term acoustical absorption, the quality of a surface or substance that takes in a sound wave rather than reflecting it.

acoustic(al)

Having to do with sound that can be heard by the ears.

acoustical absorption

The quality of a surface or substance that allows it to take in a sound wave rather than reflect it or pass it through, or an instance of this.

acoustic amplifier

The portion of an instrument that makes the vibrating source move more air or move air more efficiently, making the sound of the instrument louder. Examples of acoustic amplifiers include the body of an acoustic guitar, the soundboard of a piano, the bell of a horn and the shell of a drum.

A/D

Abbreviation of either *analogue-to-digital conversion* (ie the conversion of a quantity that has continuous changes into numbers that approximate those changes) or *analogue-to-digital converter*.

A-DAT

A trademark of Alesis for its modular digital multitrack recording system, released in early 1993.

ADSR

Abbreviation for *attack, decay, sustain* and *release*, the various elements of volume changes in the sounding of a keyboard instruments, and also the four segments of a common type of synthesiser envelope. The controls for these four parameters determine the duration (or, in the case of sustain, the height) of the segments of the envelope.

AIFF

Abbreviation of *audio interchange file format*, a common format for Macintosh audio files. It can be mono or stereo, and at a sampling rate of up to 48kHz. AIFF files are compatible with QuickTime.

algorithmic composition

A type of composition in which the large outlines of the piece, or the procedures to be used in generating it, are determined by the human composer, while some of the details, such as notes or rhythms, are created by a computer program using algorithmic processes.

aliasing

Undesired frequencies that are produced when harmonic components within the audio signal being sampled by a digital recording device or generated within a digital sound source lie above the Nyquist frequency. Aliasing differs from some other types of noise in that its pitch changes radically when the pitch of the intended sound changes. On playback, the system will provide a signal at an incorrect frequency, called an alias frequency. Aliasing is a kind of distortion.

ambience

The portion of a sound that comes from the surrounding environment, rather than directly from the sound source.

ambient field

The same as *reverberant field*, ie the area away from the sound source where the reverberation is louder than the direct sound.

ambient miking

Placing a microphone in the reverberant field in order to take a separate recording of the ambience or to allow the recording engineer to change the mix of direct to reverberant sound in the recording.

amp

1. Abbreviation of *amplifier*. 2. Abbreviation of *ampère*, the SI unit of current. 3. Abbreviation of *amplitude*, the height of a waveform above or below the zero line.

ampère

The SI unit of current, abbreviated to amp.

amplitude

The height of a waveform above or below the zero line, or the amount of a signal. Amplitude is measured by determining the amount of fluctuation in air pressure of a sound, the voltage of an electrical signal or, in a digital application, numerical data. When the signal is in the audible range, amplitude is perceived as loudness.

analogue

Representative, continuous changes that relate to another quantity that has a continuous change. Capable of exhibiting continuous fluctuations. In an analogue audio system, fluctuations in voltage correspond in a one-to-one fashion with (that is, are analogous to) the fluctuations in air pressure at the audio input or output. In an analogue synthesiser, parameters such as oscillator pitch and LFO speed are typically controlled by analogue control voltages, rather than by digital data, and the audio signal is also an analogue voltage.

analog recording

A recording of the continuous changes of an audio waveform.

analogue-to-digital converter

A device which converts a quantity that has continuous changes (usually of voltage) into numbers that approximate those changes. Alternatively, a device that changes the continuous fluctuations in voltage from an analogue device (such as a microphone) into digital information that can be stored or processed in a sampler, digital signal processor or digital recording device.

attack

The rate at which a sound begins and increases in volume.

attenuation

Making something smaller. A reduction of the strength of an electrical or acoustic signal.

aux send

Abbreviation of *auxiliary send*, which adjusts the level of a signal sent from the console input channel to the auxiliary equipment through the aux bus.

auxiliary equipment

Effects devices separate from but working with a recording console.

baffles

Sound-absorbing panels used to prevent sound waves from entering or leaving a certain space.

balance

1. The relative level of two or more instruments in a mix, or the relative level of audio signals in

the channels of a stereo recording. 2. To even out the relative levels of audio signals in the channels of a stereo recording.

balanced

1. Having a pleasing amount of low frequencies when compared to mid-range frequencies and high frequencies. 2. Having a pleasing mixture of the various instrument levels in an audio recording. 3. Having a fairly equal level in each of the stereo channels. 4. A method of interconnecting electronic gear using three-conductor cables.

bandwidth

1. The range of frequencies over which a tape recorder, amplifier or other audio device is useful. 2. The range of frequencies affected by an equalisation setting – ie the available "opening" through which information can pass. In audio, the bandwidth of a device is the portion of the frequency spectrum that it can handle without significant degradation taking place. In digital communications, the bandwidth is the amount of data that can be transmitted over a given period of time.

bank

1. A collection of sound patches (data concerned with the sequence and operating parameters of the synthesiser generators and modifiers) in computer memory. 2. A number of sound modules grouped together as a unit.

baud rate

Informally, the number of bits of computer information transmitted each second. MIDI transmissions have a baud rate of 31,250 (31.25 kilobaud), while modems typically have a much lower rate of 2,400, 9,600 or 14,400 baud.

barrier miking

A method of placing the head of a microphone as close as possible to a reflective surface, thus preventing phase cancellation.

basic session

The first session in recording an audio production to record the basic tracks.

bass roll-off

An electrical network built into some microphones to reduce the amount of output at bass frequencies when close-miking.

beats per minute

The number of steady, even pulses in music occurring in one minute and therefore defining the tempo of a song.

bi-amplification

The process of having low-frequency and high-frequency speakers driven by separate amplifiers.

bi-directional pattern

A microphone pick-up pattern that has maximum pick-up directly in front and directly to the rear of the diaphragm and least pick-up at the sides.

bit

The smallest unit of digital information, representing a single zero or one. Digital audio is encoded in words that are usually eight, twelve or 16 bits long (ie the bit resolution). Each additional bit represents a theoretical improvement of about 6dB in the signal-to-noise ratio.

blending

1. A condition where two signals mix together to form one sound or give the sound of one sound source or one performance. 2. Mixing the left and right signal together slightly, which makes the instruments sound closer to the centre of the performance stage. 3. A method of panning during mixing where instruments are not panned extremely left or right.

boom

1. A hand-held, telescoping pole used to suspend a microphone above a sound source when recording dialogue in film production. 2. A telescoping support arm attached to a microphone stand which holds the microphone. 3. Loosely, a boom stand.

boost

To increase gain, especially at specific frequencies with an equaliser.

brick-wall filter

A low-pass filter at the input of an analogue-to-digital converter. Used to prevent frequencies above the Nyquist frequency from being encoded by the converter.

buffer

Memory used for the recording or editing of data before it is stored in a more permanent form.

bulk dump

Short for *system-exclusive bulk dump*, a method of transmitting data, such as the internal parameters of a MIDI device to another MIDI device.

bus(s)

A wire carrying signals somewhere. Usually fed from several sources.

cancellation

A shortening of the term *phase cancellation*, which occurs when the energy of one waveform significantly decreases the energy of another waveform because of phase relationships at or close to 180°.

capsule

1. The variable capacitor section of a condenser microphone. 2. In other types of microphone, the part of the microphone that includes the diaphragm and the active element.

cardioid pattern

A microphone pick-up pattern which picks up most sound from the front, less from the sides and the least from the back of the diaphragm.

carrier

A signal that is modulated by some other signal, as in FM synthesis.

cascade

To set and interconnect two mixers so that the stereo mixing bus(es) of a mixer feed(s) the stereo bus(es) of a second mixer.

centre frequency

That frequency of an audio signal that is boosted or attenuated the most by an equaliser with a peak equalisation curve.

chamber

1. An echo chamber, ie a room designed with very hard, non-parallel surfaces equipped with a speaker and microphone so that, when dry signals from the console are fed to the speaker, the microphone picks up a reverberation of these signals, which can then be combined with the dry signals at the console. 2. A program in a delay/reverb effects device that simulates the sound of an echo chamber.

chase

The action of a recorder or sequencer whose speed has been automatically adjusted to be in time with another recorder.

chorusing

A type of signal processing. In chorusing, a time-delayed or detuned copy of a signal is mixed with the original signal. The mixing process changes the relative strengths and phase relationships of the overtones to create a fatter, more animated sound. The simplest way to achieve chorusing is by detuning one synthesiser oscillator from another to produce a slow beating between them.

clangorous

Containing partials that aren't part of the natural harmonic series. Clangorous tones often sound like bells.

clicking

1. Pressing and immediately releasing the switch on a computer's mouse. 2. Sound made by "poorly" cut audio when a waveform is not converging well (ie not zero snap).

clip

To deform a waveform during overload.

clock signal

The signal put out by a circuit that generates the steady, even pulses or codes used for synchronisation.

close miking

A technique involving placing a microphone close to (ideally within a foot of) a sound source being recorded in order to pick up primarily the direct sound and to avoid picking up leakage or ambience.

coincident microphones (coincident pair)

An arrangement by which the heads of two microphones are placed as close as possible to each other so that the path length from any sound source to either microphone is, for all practical purposes, the same.

comb filter

1. The frequency response achieved by mixing a direct signal with a delayed signal of equal strength, especially at short delays. 2. Also loosely used to describe effects that can be achieved with comb filtering as part of the processing.

compander

1. A two-section device used in noise-reduction systems. The first section compresses the audio signal before it is recorded and the second section expands the signal after it's been recorded. 2. In Yamaha digital consoles, a signal processor that applies both compression and expansion to the same signal. Digital companding allows a device to achieve a greater apparent dynamic range with fewer bits per sample word.

compression driver

In a horn loudspeaker, a compression driver is a unit that feeds a sound-pressure wave into the throat of the horn.

compression ratio

In a compressor or limiter, the number of decibels that an input signal has to rise above a threshold to achieve one more decibel of output.

compressor

A signal-processing device that allows less fluctuation in the level of the signal above a certain adjustable or fixed level.

condenser

An old term meaning the same thing as *capacitor*, ie an electronic device that is composed of two plates separated by an insulator and can store charge. The term is still in common use when used to refer to a microphone's active element.

condenser microphone

A microphone that converts changes in sound pressure into changes in capacitance. The capacitance changes are then converted into variations in electrical voltage (ie an audio signal).

consumer format (consumer DIF)

A standard adopted by the IEC for the sending and receiving of digital audio, based on the AES Professional Interface.

contact microphone

A device that senses vibrations and puts out an audio signal proportional to the vibrations.

controller

1. Any device – for example, a keyboard, wind synth controller or pitch-bend lever – capable of producing a change in some aspect of a sound by altering the action of some other device. 2. Any of the defined MIDI data types used for controlling the ongoing quality of a sustaining tone. (Strictly speaking, MIDI continuous controllers are numbered from 0 to 127.) In many synthesisers, the controller-data category is more loosely defined in order to include pitch-bend and aftertouch data. 3. Any device generating a control voltage or signal fed to another device's control input.

corner frequency

The same as *cut-off frequency*, ie the highest or lowest frequency present in the pass band of a filter.

CPU (central processing unit)

1. The main "brain" chip of a computer, which performs the calculations and execution of instructions. 2. The main housing of a computer containing the "brain" chip, as opposed to other pieces of the computer system, such as keyboards, monitors, etc.

critical distance

The point a distance away from the sound source at which the direct sound and the reverberant sound are equal in volume.

crossfade looping

A sample-editing feature found in many samplers and most sample-editing software in which some portion of the data at the beginning of a loop is mixed with some portion of the data at the end of the same loop in order to produce a smoother transition between the end and the beginning of the loop.

crossover (crossover network)

A set of filters that "split" the audio signal into two or more bands, or two or more signals, each of which have only some of the frequencies present.

crossover frequency

1. The frequency that is the outer limit of one of the bands of a crossover. 2. In the Lexicon 480L delay/reverberation effects unit, the frequency at which the bass-frequency reverb time is in effect rather than the mid-frequency reverb time.

crosstalk

Leakage of an audio signal from an adjacent or nearby channel into a channel that isn't intended to carry the signal.

cue

1. The signal fed back to musicians over headphones. 2. To set a tape or disc so that the intended selection will immediately play when the tape machine or player is started. 3. A location point entered into a computer controlling the playback or recording of a track or tape. 4. In MCI tape machines, a term meaning the same thing as *sync playback*, where the record head is used as a playback head for those tracks already recorded.

current

The amount of electron charge passing across a point in a conductor over a certain unit of time.

cut

1. One selection (song) on a pre-recorded music format. 2. A term with the same meaning as *mute* (ie to turn off a channel or a signal). 3. To reduce the gain of a particular band of frequencies with an equaliser. 4. To deny the passing of a particular band of frequencies (said of a filter).

cut-off/turnover frequency

1. The highest or lowest frequency in the pass band of a filter. 2. The highest or lowest frequency passed by an audio device. (The cut-off frequency is usually considered to be the first frequency to be 3dB lower than a reference frequency in the middle of the device's bandwidth.)

cut-off rate/slope

The number of decibels that a filter reduces the signal for each octave past the filter's cut-off frequency (ie outside the pass band).

cycle

1. An alternation of a waveform that begins at a point, then passes through the zero line and ends up at a point with the same value and moving in the same direction as the starting point. 2. On a Solid State Logic console, a command that tells the console's computer to control the

tape machine and make it play and replay a certain section of a tape.

cycles per second

A unit used in the measure of frequency, equivalent to Hertz. Cycles per second is an outdated term that was replaced by Hertz in 1948.

cyclic redundancy checking code

A digital error-detection code used in digital recording.

D/A

Abbreviation of *digital-to-analogue converter*, a device which changes digital data numbers (digital audio signal) into discrete voltage level.

daisy chain

1. A hook-up of several devices where the audio signal has to pass through one device to reach the second and through the second device to reach the third. 2. In MIDI, a hook-up of MIDI devices where the MIDI signal has to pass though each device in order to reach the next device.

DAT

An abbreviation of *digital audio tape* and a standard format for recording digital audio on small, specially designed cassette tapes.

DAW

Abbreviation of *digital audio workstation*, a dedicated device that is both a recorder and mixer of digital audio.

dB

Abbreviation of the term *decibel*, a unit used to compare signal strengths.

dBm

1. Decibels of audio power present compared to one milliwatt of power in a 600-ohm load. 2. Very incorrectly and too-commonly-used term designating the reference voltage of .775 volts of audio signal strength, regardless of impedance.

dBSPL

The sound-pressure level present compared in decibels to the standard sound-pressure reference level representing "no" sound (ie a sound-pressure level that about 50 per cent of people would say that they couldn't hear).

dBu (dBv)

The audio voltage present compared in decibels to the level of .775 volts of audio voltage in a circuit of any impedance.

DBX

A brand of noise reduction systems, dynamic processing equipment and other audio gear.

dead

1. Used to describe an acoustically absorbent area or space. 2. A slang term for "broken".

decay

1. The rate of reduction of an audio signal generated in synthesisers from the peak level to the sustain level. (See also *ADSR*.) 2. The fade-out of the reverberation of a sound.

decibel

A unit of measurement used to indicate audio power level. Technically, a decibel is a logarithmic ratio of two numbers, which means that there is no such thing as a decibel measurement of a single signal. In order to measure a signal in decibels, you need to know what level it's referenced to. Commonly used reference levels are indicated by such symbols as dBm, dBV and dBu.

de-esser

1. The control circuit of an audio compressor or limiter that is made more sensitive to the sounds made by a person pronouncing the letter S. 2. Any device that will reduce the high-frequency energy present when the letter S is pronounced loudly.

definition

1. The quality of a sound that allows it to be distinguished from other sounds. 2. In Lexicon reverb units, a parameter that sets a decrease in reverberation density in the later part of the decay.

degauss

A term with the same meaning as *demagnetise*, ie to remove the magnetism from something.

delay

A signal that comes from a source and is then delayed by a tape machine or delay device and can then be mixed with the original (non-delayed) signal to make it sound fuller, create echo effects, etc. 1. The first stage of a five-stage DADSR envelope, which delays the beginning of the envelope's attack segment. 2. A control function that allows one of the elements in a layered sound to start later than another element. 3. A signal processor used for flanging, doubling and echo which holds its input for a period of time before passing it to the output, or the algorithm within a signal processor that creates delay.

delay effects

Any signal processing that uses delay as its basis for processing, such as echo, reverb delay and special effects, such as flanging and chorusing.

detune

1. A control that allows one oscillator to sound a slightly different pitch than another. 2. To change the pitch of one oscillator relative to another in order to produce a fuller sound.

DI

Abbreviation of *direct injection* or *direct input*.

diaphragm

The part of the microphone which moves in response to fluctuations in the sound-pressure wave.

digital controls

1. Controls that have changing number displays when the control is changed. 2. Controls that change the digital control signal information bits to change the value of some functions.

digital delay

A delay line or delay effects unit that converts audio signal into digital audio signal, delays it and then converts it back to analogue audio signal before sending it out of the unit.

digital interface format (DIF)

A specification of the number of bits, their meaning, the voltage and the type of connector used with digital audio connections.

digital multimeter

A small, hand-held, battery operated testing device that tests levels of voltage, current, resistance and continuity. The results are showed on a digital display.

digital recording

The process of converting audio signals into numbers representing the waveform and then storing these numbers.

digital signal processing

Any signal processing done after an analogue audio signal has been converted into digital audio.

digital-to-analogue converter (DAC)

A device that changes the sample words put out by a digital audio device into analogue fluctuations in voltage that can be sent to a mixer or amplifier. All digital synthesisers, samplers and effects devices have DACs (pronounced to rhyme with fax) at their outputs to create audio signals.

dip

To reduce the levels of signals in a specific band of audio frequencies.

direct

1. Using a direct pick-up. 2. Using a direct output. 3. Recording all musicians to the final two-track master without using a multitrack tape.

direct box

An electronic device utilising a transformer or amplifier to change the electrical output of an electric instrument (for example, an electric guitar) to the impedance and level usually obtained from a microphone.

direct injection

The same as *direct pick-up*.

directional pattern

1. In microphones, the same as *pick-up pattern*, ie a description or graphic display of the level that a microphone puts out in response to sounds arriving from different directions. 2. In speakers, the pattern of dispersion (the area that the sound from a speaker will cover evenly in a listening area).

direct pick-up

Feeding the signal from an electrical instrument to the recording console or tape recorder without using a microphone but instead by changing the electrical output of the instrument to the same impedance and level as a microphone.

direct sound

The sound that reaches a microphone or listener without hitting or bouncing off any obstacles.

distant miking

The technique of placing a mic far from a sound source so that reflected sound is picked up with the direct sound.

distortion

1. The audio garble that can be heard when an audio waveform has been altered, usually by the overloading of an audio device like an amplifier. 2. The similar garbled sound that can be heard when the sound-pressure level is too loud for the waveform to be accurately reproduced by the human hearing mechanism.

diversity

A system in wireless microphone receivers that switches between two or more antennae to prevent drop-outs in the audio signal.

Dolby

The name and trademark of a manufacturer of noise-reduction systems and other audio systems. These systems improve the performance and fidelity of devices that record, play back and transmit audio material.

Doppler effect

A change in frequency of a delayed signal caused by changes in the delay time while the cycle is being formed.

double

1. To record a second performance, ie double-tracking (recording a second track with a second performance closely matching the first). 2. To use a delay line with medium delay to simulate this.

driver

In a horn loudspeaker, the unit that feeds a sound-pressure wave into the throat of the horn.

drop-out

A very short absence of signal in magnetic recording, usually caused by dirt or defects in the magnetic coating of tapes and discs, or any very short loss of an audio signal.

drum machine

A sample playback unit or sound module with drum sounds that can be sequenced by an internal sequencer to play drum patterns.

dry signal

A signal consisting entirely of the original, unprocessed sound. The output of an effects device is 100 per cent dry when only the input signal is being heard, ie with none of the effects created by the processor itself, with no reverberation or ambience. The term is more loosely used to describe an audio signal free of signal processing.

DSP

Abbreviation of *digital signal processing*, ie any signal processing performed after an analogue audio signal has been convened into digital audio. Broadly speaking, all changes in sound that are produced within a digital audio device – other than those caused by the simple cutting and pasting of sections of a waveform – are created via DSP. A digital reverb is a typical DSP device.

dub

1. To copy a recording. 2. A copy of a recording. 3. A recording made in time with another recording so that the final result is a combination of the first recording and the second recording. 4. To add dialogue to a picture after the picture has been filmed or recorded on videotape.

dynamic microphone

1. A microphone in which the diaphragm moves a coil suspended in a magnetic field in order to generate an output voltage proportional to the sound-pressure level. 2. Occasionally used to

mean any microphone that has a generating element which cuts magnetic lines of force in order to produce an output, such as a dynamic microphone (definition 1) or a ribbon microphone.

dynamic (signal) processing

An automatic change in level or gain effected to change the ratio in level of the loudest audio to the softest audio.

dynamic range

1. The level difference (in decibels) between the loudest peak and the softest level of a recording, etc. 2. The level difference between the level of clipping and the noise level in an audio device or channel.

dynamics

1. The amount of fluctuation in level of an audio signal. 2. In music, the playing of instruments loudly or softly.

dynamic voice allocation

A system found on many multitimbral synthesisers and samplers that allows voice channels to be reassigned automatically to play different notes (often with different sounds) whenever required by the musical input from the keyboard or MIDI.

early reflections

1. The first echoes in a room, caused by the sound from the sound source reflecting off one surface before reaching the listener. 2. A reverb algorithm whose output consists of a number of closely spaced, discrete echoes, designed to mimic the bouncing of sound off nearby walls in an acoustic space.

echo

1. One distinct repeat of a sound caused by the sound reflecting off a surface. 2. Loosely used to mean reverberation (ie the continuing of a sound after the source stops emitting it, caused by many discrete echoes closely spaced in time).

echo chamber

1. A room designed with very hard, non-parallel surfaces and equipped with a speaker and microphone. 2. Any artificial or electronic device that simulates the reverberation created in a room.

echo return

An input of the console which brings back the echo (reverberation) signal from the echo chamber or other echo effects device.

echo send

The output of a console used to send a signal to an echo chamber or delay effects device.

echo send control

A control to send the signal from the input module to the echo chamber or effects device via the echo bus.

edit buffer

An area of memory used for making changes in the current patch. Usually the contents of the edit buffer will be lost when the instrument is switched off and a Write operation is required to move the data to a more permanent area of memory for long-term storage.

editing

1. Changing the sequence of a recording by cutting the recording tape and putting the pieces together in the new sequence with splicing tape. 2. Punching in and then punching out on one or more tracks of a multitrack tape recorder to replace previously recorded performances. 3. Changing the sequence of a digital recording's playback by using a computer program.

effects

1. An effect is a device that modifies an audio signal by adding something to the signal to change the sound. 2. Short for the term *sound effects* (sounds other than dialogue, narration or music added to film or video shots, such as door slams, wind, etc).

effects track

1. In film production, a recording of the mixdown of all of the sound effects for the film ready to be mixed with the dialogue and music. 2. In music recording, one track with a recording of effects to be added to another track of a multitrack recording.

electret condenser

A condenser microphone that has a permanently polarised (charged) variable capacitor as its sound-pressure-level sensor.

electric current

A more formal term for *current*, ie the amount of electron charge passing across a point in a conductor per unit of time.

electromagnetic induction/pick-up

The generation of electrical signal in a conductor moving in a magnetic field or being close to a changing magnetic field.

engineer

1. A technician in charge of a recording session, also called the *recording engineer*. 2. A person in possession of an engineering degree. 3. A person with sufficient experience in the field of engineering to be equivalent to the education one would receive on an engineering degree course.

envelope

1. Description of the way in which a sound or audio signal varies in intensity over time. 2. How a control voltage changes in level over time, controlling a parameter of something other than gain or audio level. The shape of a synthesiser's envelope is controlled by a set of rate (or time) and level parameters. The envelope is a control signal that can be applied to various aspects of a synth sound, such as pitch, filter cut-off frequency and overall amplitude. Usually, each note has its own envelope(s).

envelope generator

A device that generates an envelope. Also known as a *contour generator* or *transient generator*, because the envelope is a contour (shape) that is used to create some of the transient (changing) characteristics of the sound. (See *ADSR*.)

envelope tracking

Also called *keyboard tracking, key follow* or *keyboard rate scaling*. A function that changes the length of one or more envelope segments, depending on which key on the keyboard is being pressed. Envelope tracking is most often used to give the higher notes shorter envelopes and the lower notes longer envelopes, mimicking the response characteristics of percussion-activated acoustic instruments, such as guitar and marimba.

equal loudness contours

A drawing of several curves showing how loud the tones of different frequencies would have to be played for it to be said that they were of equal loudness.

equalisation

Any time that the amplitudes of audio signals at specific set of frequencies are increased or decreased more than the signals at other audio frequencies.

equipment rack

A cabinet with rails, or free-standing rails, that have holes to accept screws at standard spaces. Used to house outboard gear.

error concealment

The replacing of information in a digital audio signal to replace lost bits when the digital recording or processing system cannot verify whether the lost bits were ones or zeros but can make a good guess by comparing the known bits that were close in position to the lost bits.

error detection

The process of discovery that sonic information has been lost in a digital audio signal.

expander

A device that causes expansion of an audio signal.

expansion

The opposite of compression. For example, an expander may allow the signal to increase 2dB every time the signal input increases by 1dB.

expansion ratio

The number of decibels that the output signal will drop for every decibel that the input signal falls below the threshold.

fade

1. A gradual reduction of the level of an audio signal. 2. A gradual change of level from one preset level to another.

fader

A device to control the gain of a channel on a console, thereby determining the level of a signal in that channel.

far field

The area covering the distance from three feet away from the sound source up to the critical distance.

fat

Having more than a normal amount of signal strength at low frequencies or having more sound than normal by the use of compression or delay.

feed

To send an audio or control signal to a device.

feedback

1. The delayed signal sent back to the input of a delay line, used in repeat-echo effects. 2. The pick-up of the signal out of a channel by its input or the howling sound that this produces. 3. In an amplifier, the phase-reversed output signal sent back to its input, reducing gain but also causing distortion and noise.

feedback control

The control on a delay line or delay effects device that controls the amount of feedback present in a signal.

fidelity

The recording or reproduction quality of an audio device.

figure-eight pattern

Another name for a bi-directional pattern, a microphone design that picks up best from the front and rear of the diaphragm and not at all from the side of the diaphragm.

filter

1. A device that removes signals with frequencies above or below a certain point, known as the *cut-off frequency*. 2. An equaliser section, used in this sense because filters are used with other components to give an equaliser its frequency response characteristics. 3. The action of removing signals of some frequencies and leaving the rest. 4. A mechanical device that smoothes out speed variations in tape machines, known as a *scrape flutter filter* or, more usually, a *scrape flutter idler*.

final mix

A two-track stereo master tape mixed from the multitrack master.

FireWire

The popular name for a high-speed digital standard connection for linking up peripherals such as digital video cameras, audio components and computer devices. FireWire was originally developed by Apple Computers as a replacement for the SCSI bus. IEEE 1394 is formal name for the standard. Vendors must obtain a licence from Apple in order to use the term FireWire.

first generation

A descriptive term meaning original, as opposed to a copy.

flange

An effect caused by combining an approximately even mix of a modulated (varying) short delay with the direct signal.

flat

1. Lower in musical pitch. 2. A slang term used to describe the sensitivity to frequency of a microphone, amplifier, etc, as being even at all frequencies (usually within 2dB).

Fletcher-Munson effect

A hearing limitation shown by Fletcher Munson equal-loudness contours that, as music is lowered in volume, it's much more difficult to hear bass frequencies and somewhat harder to hear very high frequencies.

floor

1. An alternative term to *range* (ie a limit on the amount that a signal is reduced when the input signal is lowered by an expander or gate). 2. A shortening of the term *noise floor* (ie the level of noise).

flutter

1. High-frequency variations in pitch of a recorded waveform due to rapid variations in speed

of a recorder or playback machine. 2. Originally, and more formally, any variations – fast or slow – in the pitch of a recorded tone due to speed fluctuations in a recorder or playback unit.

fly in

1. To add sounds into a mix or recording that have no synchronisation. 2. An application of this is where a performance from one part of a tune is recorded and then recorded back into the recording at a different time in the recording.

foldback

A European term for the signal sent to the stage monitors in a live performance.

formant

An element in the sound of a voice or instrument that doesn't change frequency along with pitch. Can also be described as a resonant peak in a frequency spectrum. The variable formants produced by the human vocal tract are what give vowels their characteristic sound.

format

1. The number, width, spacing and order of tracks for the purposes of tape recording. 2. To prepare a digital storage medium so that it will accept and store digital information.

frame

1. The amount of time that one still picture is shown in film or video. 2. A division of one second in synchronisation and recording, coming from definition 1.

FreeMIDI

A Macintosh operating system extension developed by Mark Of The Unicorn that enables different programs to share MIDI data. For example, a sequencer could communicate with a librarian program to display synthesiser patch names – rather than just numbers – in its editing windows.

frequency

The number of cycles of a waveform occurring in the space of a second.

frequency range

The range of frequencies over which an electronic device is useful or over which a sound source puts out substantial energy.

frequency response

The measure of sensitivity shown by an electronic device (microphone, amplifier, speaker, etc) to various frequencies. Often communicated via a graph.

frequency shift key

A simple clock signal that can be used to run a sequencer in time with an audio tape.

full

Used to describe a sound that has all frequencies present, especially the low frequencies.

full step

A change in pitch that occurs when one moves up or down two piano keys.

fundamental

The tuned frequency and, almost always, the lowest frequency that is present in the sounding of a pitch by a musical instrument.

gain

An increase in the strength of an audio signal, often expressed in decibels.

gain control

A device that changes the gain of an amplifier or circuit. Often appears as a knob that can be turned or a slider that can be moved up and down.

gain reduction

A reduction in gain during high-level passages, effected by a limiter or compressor.

gain structure

The way in which gain changes at the various stages or sections of an audio system.

gate

A dynamics-processing device that turns a channel off or down when a signal drops below a certain level.

General MIDI (GM)

A set of requirements adopted by manufacturers of MIDI devices and used to ensure the consistent playback performance on all instruments bearing the GM logo. Some of the requirements include 24-voice polyphony and a standardised group and location of sounds. For example, patch 17 will always be a drawbar organ sound on all General MIDI instruments.

generating element

The portion of a microphone that actually converts the movement of the diaphragm into electrical current or changes in voltage.

generation

A term used here to describe the number of times that a recorded audio signal has been copied.

generation loss

The amount of clarity lost in an audio copy due to added noise and distortion.

glide

A function where the pitch slides smoothly from one note to the next instead of jumping over the intervening pitches. Also called *portamento*.

golden section

A ratio of exact height to width to length of a room in order to achieve good acoustics. First recommended by the ancient Greeks. The ratio is approximately the width of a room x 1.6 times its height and its length x 2.6 times its height.

gigabyte

One billion bytes.

global

Pertaining to or governing all of the operations of an instrument.

graphic editing

A method of editing parameter values using graphical representations (for example, of envelope shapes) displayed on a computer screen or LCD.

graphic equaliser

A device equipped with several slides to control the gain of an audio signal present within one of several evenly spaced frequency bands, spaced according to octaves.

ground

US equivalent of British *earth*. In electronics, a place (terminal) that has zero volts.

ground lift

A switch that breaks the connection between the ground points in two different circuits.

ground lifter

An adapter that takes a three-pronged power cord and plugs into a two-pronged outlet, used to disconnect the third (ground) pin of the power outlet. It can be *very* dangerous to have no ground connection to the casing by using a ground lifter and not grounding the unit by other means.

ground loop

A double grounding of a line or electronic device at two different "ground" points of differing voltage.

group

1. A number of channels or faders that can be controlled by one master VCA slide. 2. A shortening of the term *recording group* (ie a bus or the signal present on a bus).

group faders

The VCA faders of a number of individual channels that are all controlled by a group master fader (ie a slide control used to send out a control voltage to several VCA faders in individual channels).

grouping

1. Controlling the gain of several individual channels with a group fader. 2. The mixing together of several individual audio signals to send a mixed signal out of the console to record a track on a multitrack tape machine.

group master

A slide control used to send out a control voltage to several VCA faders in individual channels, thus controlling the gain of several channels.

Haas effect

Simply stated, a factor in human hearing where delay has a much bigger effect on the human perception of direction than level does.

half step

A difference in pitch present between adjacent keys on a piano.

hall program

A setting of a digital delay/reverb effects unit that approximates concert halls. Hall programs are characterised by a pre-delay of up to 25ms.

harmonic

A frequency that is a whole-number multiple of the fundamental frequency. For example, if the fundamental frequency of a sound is 440Hz, the first two harmonics are 880Hz and 1,320Hz (1.32kHz). Harmonics are whole-number multiples of the frequency that determines the timbre recognition of an instrument's sound.

harmonic distortion

The presence of harmonics in the output signal of a device that weren't present in the input signal.

head amp

Alternative name for pre-amplifier, a low-noise amplifier designed to take a low-level signal, such as the output of a tape head, and bring it up to normal line level.

headphones

Devices that can be worn on the head fitted with small speakers that fit over the ears or, sometimes, into the ears.

headroom

1. The level difference (in decibels) between normal operating level and clipping level in an amplifier or audio device. 2. A similar level difference between normal tape-operating level and the level at which the distortion would be three per cent.

hearing limitation

An inability of the human ear to hear important characteristics of sound under certain conditions. Characteristics that can be affected include pitch, level, clarity, presence and direction.

hertz

The basic unit of frequency, equivalent to *cycles per second*. The term is usually abbreviated to Hz.

high frequencies

Audio frequencies at 6,000Hz and above.

high impedance

Impedance of 5,000 ohms or more.

high-impedance mic

A microphone designed to be fed into an amplifier with an input impedance greater than 20,000 ohms.

high-pass filter

A device that rejects signals below a certain frequency (known as the *cut-off frequency*) and passes signals with frequencies that are higher than this.

hi-Z

Abbreviation of *high impedance* (ie an impedance of 5,000 ohms or more).

horn

A speaker or speaker enclosure where sound-pressure waves are fed through a narrow opening (by a speaker cone or driver) and where the narrow opening flares out into a larger opening.

hum

Produced when 60Hz power-line current is accidentally induced or fed into electronic equipment.

hypercardioid pattern

A microphone pick-up sensitivity pattern demonstrating that the least-sensitive pick-up point is more than 90° but less than 150° off axis (usually 120°).

Hz

Abbreviation of *Hertz*, the unit of frequency.

ID

An index signal (ie digital data that provides a machine with information concerning the starting points and selection numbers of sections, etc) on a DAT or CD.

IM distortion

Abbreviation of *intermodulation distortion*, which is caused by one signal beating with another signal and producing frequencies that are both the sum and the difference of the original frequencies present.

impedance

The opposition to alternating current (AC).

impedance matching

Having or converting the output impedance of a device so that it matches the impedance of the input that it will feed.

in

Short for "in the circuit". In other words, active.

in-line console

A console equipped with modules that have all of the controls for all of the sections in one long strip.

infinite baffle

A baffle so large that the sounds coming from one side don't reach the other.

infinite repeat

A function on some delay lines that cause enough feedback for the repeat echo to last forever but not enough to cause a howling sound.

information bits

The bits in a digital signal that make up actual values or commands being communicated, as opposed to those bits that are used for the checking and correction of data or for other purposes.

inharmonic

Containing frequencies that are not whole-number multiples of the fundamental.

in port

A jack on a MIDI device or computer that will accept an incoming data signal.

input

1. The jack or physical location of the point at which a device receives a signal. 2. A signal being received by a device. 3. To feed a signal from one device to another.

input impedance

The opposition to current flow exerted by the first circuits of a device.

input/output module

A set of controls on one housing for an in-line console that has two channels – one for recording and one for monitoring – and which has controls for all console sections.

input overload

Sending too high a signal level into a device, so that the first amplifier of the device overloads.

insert

1. A punch in performed on all of the tracks being recorded in a recording session. 2. On Solid State Logic consoles, to place an outboard piece of gear in a channel by patching and activating a switch.

instrument amplifier

A device that has a power amplifier and speaker in a case (or in separate cases) to reproduce the signal put out by an electric instrument (such as an electric guitar) and to allow the instrument to be heard.

instrument out direct

The action of feeding the output of an electric instrument, such as an electric guitar, to a recording console or tape recorder without using a microphone.

intermodulation distortion

Form of distortion caused by one signal beating with another signal and producing frequencies that are both the sum and the difference of the original frequencies.

inverse square law

This expresses the fact that, in an unobstructed area (such as an open field), the sound-pressure level will drop to half pressure (-6dB) every time the distance to a sound source is doubled.

I/O

Abbreviation of *input/output*, referring to: 1. an in-line console module that contains controls for the input section, output section and monitor section; 2. a module in electronic gear containing input and output amplifiers for the device; and 3. a digital port (connector) able to both receive digital data and output digital data.

isolation

A containing of the sound wave in a certain area so that it won't leak into other areas and/or unintended mics.

isolation booth/room

A room that prevents loud sounds produced by other instruments from leaking in. An isolation booth is usually too small to be used by more than one musician.

jack

A connector mounted on the casing of a device or on a panel.

jack bay

A series of jacks that have connections for most of the inputs and outputs of the equipment in a control room.

jam sync

A generation of new SMPTE according to the input SMPTE signal.

key

The control of a dynamics-processing device via an external audio signal.

keyboard scaling

A function by which the sound can be altered smoothly across the range of a keyboard by using key numbers as a modulation source. Level scaling changes the loudness of the sound, while filter scaling changes its brightness.

keying input/key input

An input on a dynamics-processing device used to control the device via an external audio signal.

key note number

A number assigned to each key of a synthesiser or controller keyboard that is transmitted in the MIDI signal.

kHz

Abbreviation of *kiloHertz* (1,000 Hertz).

kilo

A prefix meaning 1,000.

kilobyte (KB)

Linguistically, 1,000 bytes. In practice, a kilobyte generally contains 1,024 bytes.

layering

The recording or playing of a musical part with several similar sound patches playing simultaneously.

lead sheet

A written chart showing the melody, lyrics and chords of a tune, complete with musical notation.

leakage

Sounds from other instruments and sources that weren't intended to be picked up by a mic.

LED (light-emitting diode)

A light that allows current to flow in one direction only and emits light whenever a voltage of a certain level or beyond is applied to it.

level

The amount of signal strength (ie the amplitude, especially the average amplitude).

LFO (low-frequency oscillator)

An oscillator that puts out an AC signal between .1Hz and 10Hz, used for a control signal. Especially devoted to applications below the audible frequency range, and typically used as a control source for modulating a sound to create vibrato, tremolo, trills and so on.

lift

To boost the gain of an audio signal at a particular band of frequencies with an equaliser.

limiter

A device that reduces gain when the input voltage exceeds a certain level.

line

1. Abbreviation of *line level*. 2. A cable.

linear

The condition of obtaining a change at the output of the device which is proportional to the change occurring at the input.

line input

An input designed to take a line-level signal.

link

A term used with reference to compressors and dynamic-processing units meaning to combine the control input signals of two channels of a compressor (or dynamic-processing unit) so that both channels always have the same gain and are triggered to change gain by the signal of either channel.

listen circuits

A type of solo circuit that allows you to listen to a channel before the fader or after the fader.

live

1. Refers to the sound produced by instruments during a performance to an audience. 2. Having a large portion of reverberant or reflected sound.

live recording

1. The practice of recording where all musicians are playing at once and no overdubbing takes place. 2. Recorded material with a lot of natural reverberation.

lo-Z

Abbreviation for the term Low Impedance (Impedance of 500 ohms or less).

load

1. The opposition to an audio output signal of a device by the input of the device being fed. 2. A resistor that would have the lowest impedance that a device was designed to feed into used during the testing of a device. 3. To copy the digital data on a storage medium into the RAM of a computer. 4. To put tape onto a tape machine and activate the computer-controlled constant-tension system.

load impedance

The opposition to the flow of output current caused by the input that it feeds.

local (mode) on/off

A switch or function in a synthesiser that connects (On) or disconnects (Off) the keyboard control of the synthesiser's sound module.

long delay

Delay times greater than 60ms.

loop

1. The same as *anti-node*, ie the points of maximum displacement of motion in a vibrating, stretched string. 2. A piece of material that plays over and over. In a sequencer, a loop repeats a musical phrase. In a sampler, loops are used to allow samples of finite length to be sustained indefinitely.

loudness

A measure of how loud something sounds to the ear.

loudness control

A knob that changes the level and adjusts the frequency response of the circuit controlling the speakers in order to compensate for the inability of the ear to hear low frequencies and extremely high frequencies at low volumes.

low end

A slang term for bass-frequency signals (ie those below 250Hz).

low frequencies

1. Audio or audible frequencies below 1kHz. 2. The range of bass frequencies below approximately 250Hz.

low impedance

Impedance of 500 ohms or less.

low-pass filter

A device that rejects signals above a certain frequency and passes those that are lower in frequency.

magnetic

1. Emitting magnetic energy. 2. Able to be magnetised.

magnetic lines of force

The magnetic field that exists between poles of a magnet.

map

A table in which input values are arbitrarily assigned to outputs by the user on an item-by-item basis.

mapper

A device that translates MIDI data from one form to another in real time.

margin

The amount of decibels between the highest peak level of a program and the point at which overload occurs.

masking

The characteristic of hearing by which loud sounds prevent the ear from hearing softer sounds of similar frequency.

master

1. A control to set the level going out of a console, especially the stereo output to a two-track machine at mixdown. 2. A term with the same meaning as *sub-master*, ie a control that adjusts the level of a signal mixed together and sent out to one track of a multitrack recorder. 3. A term with the same meaning as *VCA master*, ie one slider that controls the control voltage sent to several VCA faders. 4. A machine used as a speed reference when synchronising two or more machines to run together. If the master tape transport changes speed, the other machines synced to it will change speed with it. 5. The original recording, used for making copies. 6. To make an original recording which will be used to make commercial copies, especially making a master lacquer (for record manufacturing) or a master CD.

master fader

1. The fader which controls the main output(s) of a console during mixdown. 2. In some consoles, faders which control outputs to a multitrack tape recorder during recording. 3. Occasionally used to mean a VCA master (ie one slide that controls the control voltage sent to several VCA faders).

MCI

Abbreviation of *media control interface*, a multimedia specification designed to provide control of onscreen movies and peripherals, such as CD-ROM drives.

MDM

Abbreviation of the term *modular digital multitrack*, ie a multitrack digital recorder with (usually) eight tracks that can be run in synchronisation with other machines (of the same type) in order to attain more tracks. An example of this type of machine is the A-DAT (Alesis' modular digital multitrack recording system).

measure

The grouping of a number of beats in music.

medium delay

Delay times of 20-60ms.

meg(a)

1. A prefix for 1,000,000. 2. A slang abbreviation of megaHertz (1,000,000Hz) or megabytes (1,024,000 bytes).

memory

The components in a computer or devices that can be connected to a computer that store digital data. In the case of musical devices, this data comprises information about patches, sequences, waveforms and so on.

merger

A MIDI accessory that allows two incoming MIDI signals to be combined into one MIDI output.

meter

A device which measures or compares electrical signals, often used to read the voltage levels of audio signals.

mic

Abbreviation of *microphone*.

mic gain control

A level control on a mic pre-amp that sets gain and is used to prevent the overload of that pre-amp.

mic input

The input of a console or other device into which a microphone can be plugged.

mic level

The very low audio voltage level that comes out of a studio microphone.

mic/line switch

The selector switch on the input of a console channel that chooses which input jack feeds the console.

mic pad

A device that reduces the level of a signal, placed just before a microphone pre-amplifier to prevent overloading of the pre-amplifier.

mic pre-amp

An amplifier that boosts the low-level audio signal produced by a microphone up to line level.

microphone

A transducer that converts sound-pressure waves into electrical signals.

microprocessor

One IC (Integrated Circuit) that performs the core of activities in a computer.

MIDI

Abbreviation of *musical instrument digital interface*, a digital signal system (ie a system of number signals) used to send and receive performance information to and from musical instruments.

MIDI channel

A grouping of data concerning the performance of one synthesiser or device separate from the data concerning other synthesisers or devices. MIDI commands contain all of the information that a sound board needs to reproduce the desired sound.

MIDI clock

Time data in a MIDI signal that advances one step each $1/24$ of a beat and can be used to sync two sequencers together.

MIDI clock with song pointer

A MIDI clock signal (ie time data in the MIDI signal that advances one step each $1/24$ of a beat) that has a number signal for each measure to indicate the number of measures into a tune.

MIDI controller

A device that can be played by a musician that transmits MIDI signals to control synthesisers or sound modules.

MIDI echo

A function in a synthesiser that causes the output of a sequencer to send a MIDI signal out of the out port matching the MIDI signal coming in for the track being recorded.

MIDI interface

A device that converts a MIDI signal into the digital format used by a computer so that the computer can store and use the MIDI signal.

MIDI mode

Any of the ways in which devices respond to incoming MIDI data. While four modes – Omni Off/Poly, Omni On/Poly, Omni Off/Mono and Omni On/Mono – are defined by the MIDI specification, Omni On/Mono is never used. There are also at least two other useful modes that have been developed: Multi mode, for multitimbral instruments, and Multi-Mono mode, for guitar synthesisers.

MIDI patch bay

A device that has several MIDI inputs and outputs and allows any input to be routed to any output.

MIDI sample dump

The copying of a digitally recorded sample without converting it to analogue between different storage units or sound modules through a MIDI transmission.

MIDI sequencer

A computer that can record and play back MIDI data in such a way as to be able to control the performance of MIDI-controlled musical instruments or devices in a series of timed steps.

MIDI thru

There are two types of MIDI Thru. One, a simple hardware connection, is found on the back panels of many synthesisers. This Thru jack simply duplicates whatever data is arriving at the MIDI In jack. Sequencers have a second type, called Software Thru, where data arriving at the In jack is merged with data being played by the sequencer, and both sets of data appear in a single stream at the Out (rather than the Thru) jack. Software Thru is useful because it allows you to hook a master keyboard to the sequencer's MIDI In and a tone module to its Out. You can then play the keyboard and hear the tone module, and the sequencer can also send its messages directly to the tone module.

MIDI time code

All of the information contained in SMPTE time code that has been converted into part of the MIDI signal.

mid-range frequencies

Audio frequencies from around 250Hz through to 6,000Hz.

milli

A prefix meaning a thousandth – for example, milliwatt.

MiniDisc

A small, recordable compact disc that can be used by general consumers, introduced by Sony at the end of 1992.

mix

1. To blend audio signals together into a composite signal. 2. The signal made by blending individual signals together. 3. A control or function on a delay/reverberation device that controls the amount of direct signal that is mixed into the processed signal.

mix down

To combine the signals from the tracks of a multitrack tape onto a master tape. Reverberation and other effects may be also added.

mixer

1. A console or other device that blends audio signals into composite signals and has a small number of outputs. 2. A section on a console that performs this function. 3. In Europe, a fader. 4. An engineer or technician who mixes, especially a live-sound mix during a live performance.

mixing console/desk

A device that can combine several signals into one or more composite signals in any proportion.

mixing solo

A button that turns off all other channels, thus allowing the signal to be heard in the stereo perspective and the level used at mixdown, and with reverberation also applied.

modulation

The control of one signal by another AC signal.

modulation noise

Noise that is present only when the audio signal is present.

module

A group of circuits and controls that are mounted on a removable housing. On consoles, this often means all of the controls and circuits for one or two channels.

monitor

1. To listen, in the context of audio. 2. To indicate with a meter or light the conditions in a circuit, especially level and overload. 3. A device designed to listen or observe.

monitor mixer

1. A console or other device that blends audio signals into composite signals and has a small number of outputs. 2. The section of a console that is used to complete a rough mix so that an engineer can hear what's being recorded without effecting the levels being fed to the multitrack recorder. 3. The audio technician who mixes the signals sent to the stage monitor speakers.

monitor pot

A rotary control used to set the level of the track signal in the monitor (ie the signal to or the signal back from one track of a multitrack tape recorder).

monitor (mixer) section

The section of a console that is used to complete a rough mix so that an engineer can hear what's being recorded without effecting the levels being fed to the multitrack recorder.

monitor selector

1. On consoles, a switch that allows you to hear various things over the control-room monitor speakers, such as the main console outputs (for mixing purposes), the monitor mixer section (for recording and overdubbing), the disc player, tape machines and other devices. 2. On tape machines, a switch that, in one position, sends the signal from the tape to the meters and the output of the machine's electronics or, in a second position, sends the input signal being fed to the machine to the meters and the outputs of the electronic devices.

mono

Abbreviation of *monophonic*.

monophonic

1. More formal term for mono and meaning that there is only one sound source, or that the signal was derived from one sound source. 2. In synthesisers, a term meaning that only one pitch may be sounded at a time.

moving-coil microphone

The same as *dynamic microphone*, ie a mic in which the diaphragm moves a coil suspended in a magnetic field in order to generate an output voltage proportional to the sound-pressure level.

moving-fader automation

In consoles, a feature that enables an engineer to program changes in fader levels so that these changes happen automatically upon playback of a multitrack recording, because the fader positions actually change. The faders are driven by tiny motors.

ms

Abbreviation of *milliseconds* (thousandths of a second). Not usually capitalised.

ms miking

A method of placing stereo microphones so that one cardioid microphone points directly at the middle of the area to be miked and a bi-directional microphone is as close as possible to the first mic, with its rejection pointing the same way as the axis of the first mic.

MTC

Abbreviation of *MIDI time code*, ie all of the information of SMPTE time code that has been converted into part of the MIDI signal.

multi(jack)

Abbreviation of the term *multiple jack(s)*. 1. A jack at the output of a device which is not normalised so that plugging into the jack socket will allow the output to be sent to a different input and the output will also feed the place that it normally it feeds. 2. A set of jacks (or one of a set of jacks) with each terminal wired to a corresponding terminal of another or other jacks.

multi mode

A MIDI reception mode in which a multitimbral module responds to MIDI input on two or more channels and maintains musical independence between the channels, typically playing a different patch on each channel.

multisample

The distribution of several related samples at different pitches across a keyboard. Multisampling can provide greater realism in sample playback (wavetable) synthesis, since the individual samples don't have to be transposed over a great distance.

multitasking

The running of more than one program at the same time by a computer.

multitimbral

A synthesiser that is able to send out several signals of different sound patches (and often playing different parts) or has several sound modules is said to be multitimbral.

multitrack recording

1. Recording various instruments separately on different portions of the same tape in time with each other so that final balancing of the sound may be accomplished later. 2. Digitally recording various instruments onto a hard disk in different data files so that they may be played in time with each other and so that the final balancing of the sound may be accomplished later.

multitrack tape

A magnetic tape that can be used to store two or more discrete signals in time with each other.

mute switch

A switch that turns off a channel, takes out a track signal from the monitors or turns off the entire monitor signal.

nanowebers per metre

The standard unit in measuring magnetic energy.

narrow-band noise

Noise (random energy) produced over a limited range of frequencies.

near field

The area up to one foot away from the sound source.

negative feedback

Used to describe an out-of-phase portion of an output signal that is fed into the input of an amplifier.

noise

1. Random energy that contains energy at all audio frequencies. 2. Any unintentional or objectionable signal added to an audio signal.

noise filter

A filter that passes only signals with the intended audio frequencies, thus eliminating noise signals at other frequencies.

noise floor

The level of noise below the signal, measured in decibels.

noise gate

A gate used to turn off an audio channel when noise but no signal is present.

noise reduction

Any device designed to remove noise in a device or system.

non-directional

With mics, the same thing as *omni-directional* (ie picking up sound from all directions).

non-linear

The condition of obtaining a change at the output of the device that is not proportional to the change occurring at the input, therefore causing distortion.

normalise

1. To provide normalised switches on a jack. 2. To reset a synthesiser, sound module or sample-playback unit to the original factory settings. 3. To adjust the level of a selection so that the highest peak is at the maximum recording level of the medium. 4. To boost the level of a waveform to its maximum amount without experiencing clipping (distortion), thus maximising resolution and minimising certain types of noise.

normalising jacks (normals)

Switches on patch jacks that connect certain jack sockets together until a patch cord is inserted.

notch

A narrow band of audio frequencies.

notch filter

A device that rejects signals that have frequencies within a narrow band of audio frequencies and passes all other signals.

null

1. A condition of zero energy or movement. 2. In console automation, the position of a slide or fader at the exact point at which it was originally positioned when the automated mix was made.

nW/m

Abbreviation of *nanowebers per meter*, the standard unit in measuring amounts of magnetic energy.

nybble

Half a byte (ie four information bits).

Nyquist frequency

The highest frequency that can be recorded and reproduced properly by a particular sampling rate. Theoretically, the Nyquist frequency is half of the sampling rate. For example, when a digital recording uses a sampling rate of 44.1kHz, the Nyquist frequency is 22.05kHz. If a signal being sampled contains frequency components that are above the Nyquist frequency, aliasing will be introduced in the digital representation of the signal, unless those frequencies are filtered out prior to digital encoding.

Nyquist rate

The lowest sampling rate that can be used to record and reproduce a given audio frequency.

octave

A difference of pitch where one tone has a frequency that is double or half that of another tone.

off axis

1. Away from the front or axis of the mic. Measured in degrees. 2. 180° from the front.

offset/offset time

1. SMPTE time that triggers a MIDI sequencer. 2. The amount of position difference needed to get two reels to play music in time.

omni

A prefix meaning "all".

omni-directional

1. Used to describe microphones that pick up evenly from all directions. 2. Used to describe speakers that send out evenly in all directions.

omni mode

When Omni mode is activated in a MIDI device, all MIDI messages are recognising and acted on, no matter what their channel.

OMS

Abbreviation of *open music system* (formerly *Opcode MIDI system*), a real-time MIDI operating system for Macintosh applications. OMS allows communication between different MIDI programs and hardware so that, for example, a sequencer could interface with a librarian program to display synthesiser patch names in the sequencer's editing windows, rather than just numbers.

on axis

The position directly in front of the diaphragm of a microphone, in line with its direction of movement.

op amp

Abbreviation of the term *operational amplifier*, an amplifying circuit used in most audio devices.

open circuit

1. A break in a conductor or an incomplete path of electron flow for some other reason. 2. Said of an amplifier that has nothing feeding the input.

operating level

The maximum level of operation, which should not be exceeded.

operational amplifier

An amplifying circuit used in most audio devices.

oscillator

1. A device that puts out test tones at various frequencies in order to align a tape machine or for other testing purposes. 2. In a digital synth, an oscillator more typically plays back a complex waveform by reading the numbers in a wave table.

outboard equipment

Equipment that is used with, but is not part of, a console.

out of phase

1. Being similar to another signal in amplitude, frequency and wave shape but being offset in time by part of a cycle. 2. Having the opposite polarity (ie being 180° out of phase).

out port

A jack that sends out digital data from a computer or digital device.

output

1. The jack or physical location at which a device sends out a signal. 2. The signal put out by a device.

output impedance

The opposition to current flow by the output circuits of an amplifier or some other device.

output level

The signal level at the output of a device.

output selector

The switch on a tape machine which, when activated, allows the VU meter and audio output of the circuits of a tape machine to monitor and send out either the input signal to the tape machine, the playback of what was being recorded or the level of bias currently being fed to the record head.

overdub

To record additional parts alongside or merged with previous tracks. Overdubbing enables "one-man band" productions, as multiple synchronised performances are recorded sequentially.

Over-Easy

DBX's trademark term for the gradual change of compression ratio around the threshold, thus making it difficult to detect when compression is taking place.

overload

To put out too much signal level, thereby causing distortion.

overload indicator

An LED on a console channel that lights up when the input or some other part of the circuit is receiving an overload.

oversampling

A process where the analogue audio (or the digital audio, for playback) is sampled many times more than the minimum sampling rate.

overtones

The harmonics of an instrument's sound minus the fundamental frequency.

pad

1. An attenuator usually used to prevent the overloading of the amplifier that follows it. 2. A device with a surface that can be hit by a drum stick, whereby hitting the pad produces an output signal pulse (or MIDI command) which causes a drum machine or synthesiser to produce a drum sound.

pan pot

An electrical device that distributes one audio signal to two or more channels or speakers.

parallel

1. A circuit interconnection where the source feeds several branched circuit components and

where interrupting the current flow in one component doesn't stop current flow in another. 2. A method of sending data where each digit of a digital word is sent at the same time over separate connections.

parallel jacks

Several jacks that are wired together so that each connection is wired to the corresponding connection of other jacks.

parallel port

A jack that sends out or receives digital data where several bits are being sent or received at the same time through different pins.

parameter

A user-adjustable quantity that governs an aspect of a device's performance. Normally, the settings of all of the parameters that make up a synthesiser patch can be changed by the user and stored in memory, but the parameters themselves are defined by the operating system and can't be altered.

parametric EQ

An equaliser in which all of the parameters of equalisation can be adjusted to any amount, including centre frequency, the amount of boost or cut in gain and bandwidth.

partial

1. In acoustic instruments, a term with the same meaning as *overtone*. 2. In synthesisers, the term means literally "part of a sound patch", ie circuitry in the synthesiser that generates and/or modifies elements of a sound in order to provide a particular tone with timbre. 3. The sound element generated by definition 2.

pass band

The frequency range of signals that will be passed by a filter, rather than reduced by it.

passive device

A piece of signal-processing gear or other device that doesn't use an amplifier as part of its design.

patch

To connect together – as in the inputs and outputs of various modules – generally with patch cords. Also applied to the configuration of hook-ups and settings that results from the process of patching and, by extension, the sound that such a configuration creates. Often used to denote a single tone colour or the contents of a memory location that contains parameter settings for such a tone colour, even on an instrument that requires no physical patching.

patch bay

A series of jacks with connections for most of the inputs and outputs of a console, the console sections, tape machines and other pieces of equipment.

patch editor

A computer program that allows the user to either create or change sound patch parameters, thereby creating or modifying a specific synthesised sound outside a synthesiser.

patch field

A series of jacks that has connections for most of the inputs and outputs of the console, console sections, tape machines and other pieces of equipment.

patch lead

A cable with two plugs on it used to interconnect two patch jacks in the patch bay.

patch librarian

A computer program that allows the storing of sound patches outside a synthesiser.

patch map

A map with which any incoming MIDI Program Change message can be assigned to call up any of an instrument's patches (sounds).

patch panel

A series of jacks with connections for most of the inputs and outputs of the console, console sections, tape machines and other pieces of equipment.

patch point

One jack in a patch bay.

path

Short for *signal path*, the course that current follows or may follow in a circuit or across a device.

PCM

Abbreviation of *pulse-code modulation*, ie the use of amplitude pulses in magnetic tape to record the digital information bits comprising digital audio data.

peak

1. The highest point in an audio waveform. 2. Short for *peak detecting* (ie responding to a peak) or *peak indicating* (ie showing a peak). 3. Having a frequency response that would draw something similar to a mountain peak on a frequency response graph.

peak detecting

Recognising and responding to peak values of a waveform, rather than average values.

peak indicating meter

A meter that reads the absolute peak level of a waveform.

peaking filter

An EQ circuit which exhibits a peak response.

peak level

The same as *peak value*, ie the maximum positive or negative instantaneous value of a waveform.

peak responding

Recognising and responding to (or indicating) a peak value, rather than the average or effective value.

peak response

1. The same as *peak*. 2. A raising or lowering of the amplitude of signals at the centre frequency more than signals at any other frequency.

peak-to-peak value

The difference in amplitude between positive and negative peaks. Equal to twice the peak value for a sine wave.

peak value

The maximum positive or negative instantaneous value of a waveform.

percentage quantization

A method of quantization by which notes recorded into a sequencer with uneven rhythms aren't shifted all the way to their theoretically perfect timings but are instead shifted part of the way, with the degree of shift being dependent on a user-selected percentage (quantization strength). (See *quantization*.)

phantom powering

A system used to supply condenser microphones with power, thus eliminating the need for external power supplies.

phase cancellation

Phase cancellation occurs when the energy of one waveform decreases the energy of another waveform because of phase relationships at or close to 180°.

phase distortion

A change in a sound because of a phase shift in the signal.

phase-distortion synthesis

A method of altering a wave shape in order to add harmonics by phase-shifting while a cycle is being formed.

phase lock

1. A method of keeping tape machines synced together by sensing phase differences in the playback of pilot tunes by the two machines and adjusting their speeds to eliminate the phase difference. 2. In synthesisers, the control of one tone generator so that it begins its waveform in phase with the signal from another tone generator.

phase reversal

A change in a circuit effected in order to cause a waveform to shift by 180°.

phase shift

A delay introduced into an audio signal, measured in degrees delayed.

phase sync

1. The same as *phase lock*. 2. A method of keeping machines synced together by sensing phase differences in the playback of pilot tones by the two machines and adjusting their speeds to eliminate the phase difference.

phasing

An effect sound created by the variable phase-shifting of an audio signal mixed with the direct signal.

phon

1. A unit of equal loudness for all audio frequencies. 2. The phon is numerically equal to dBSPL (Sound-Pressure Level) at 1,000Hz but varies at other frequencies according to ear sensitivity.

phono cartridge

1. A device which changes the mechanical vibrations stored on records into electrical signals. 2. A transducer that changes sound stored as mechanical vibrations to sound in the form of electricity.

phone plug (jack)

A plug (or its mating jack) with a diameter of a quarter of an inch and a length of one and a quarter inches used for interconnecting audio devices.

pick-up

1. A device on an electric guitar (or other instrument) that puts out an audio signal according to the motion of the strings on the instrument. 2. A device that puts out an audio signal according to the vibration of something. This term means the same thing as *contact microphone*.

pick-up pattern

The shape of the area from which a microphone will evenly pick up sound, giving similar but less detailed information than a polar pattern.

pilot tone

1. The same as *neo-pilot tone*. 2. A system of recording a 60Hz tone, used for syncing on a quarter-inch tape developed by Nagra.

pink noise

Noise that has equal energy per octave or portion of an octave.

pin plug

1. The same as *RCA plug*. 2. A common audio connector found on most stereo systems, with a centre pin as one connection and an outer shell as the second connection.

pitch

1. The ear's perception of frequency (ie music sounding higher or lower). 2. A control on a tape machine which increases or decreases speed slightly, thus changing the pitch and time of the music. 3. The spacing of the grooves on a phonographic record.

pitch bend

1. In a synthesiser, the pitch-bend control makes the pitch smoothly glide upwards slightly. 2. The wheel controller or MIDI command used to bring this about.

pitch change

1. A characteristic of human hearing where bass frequencies sound lower in pitch at high levels of sound pressure, often as much as ten per cent lower. 2. A function of a delay device where the pitch of the output signal is different to that of the input signal.

pitch ratio

The percentage of pitch change in a delay line's pitch-change program.

pitch shift

To change the pitch of a sound without changing its duration, as opposed to *pitch transpose*, which changes both. Some people use the two terms interchangeably.

pitch-to-MIDI converter

A device that converts audio signals into MIDI information.

pitch-to-voltage converter

A device that converts the frequency changes of audio signals into proportional voltage changes.

plate

1. A type of reverb device in which a large metal sheet is suspended on spring clips and driven like a speaker cone. 2. An electrode in a tube that receives electrons.

plate program

A setting in a digital delay/reverb device that simulates the sound of plate reverberation.

playback equalisation

A reduction of the amplitude of those signals with high frequencies during the playback of a tape in order to compensate for the record equalisation.

playback level

1. The same as *reproduction level*. 2. A control that determines the output levels of signals played back from recorded tracks.

playlist

A series of computer commands sent to a disk recording of digital audio material where the playback of the digital audio is to comprise certain portions of the material and not others.

plug

A connector (usually on a cable) that mates with a jack.

plug-in

A software program that acts as an extension to a larger program, adding new features.

point source

A design in speaker systems where separate speakers are made, reproducing different frequency ranges, so that the sound appears to come from one place.

polarising voltage

Voltage applied to the plates of the variable capacitor in a condenser microphone capsule.

polarity

The direction of current flow or magnetising force.

polar pattern

1. A graphic display of the audio output levels caused by sound waves arriving at a microphone from different directions. 2. A graphic display of a speaker's dispersion pattern.

pole mode

A MIDI mode that allows voices of controlled synth to be assigned polyphonically by incoming key-note numbers. The more poles a filter has, the more abrupt its cut-off slope. Each pole causes a slope of 6dB per octave. Typical configurations are two-pole and four-pole (12dB and 24dB per octave).

polyphonic

Used to describe a device capable of producing more than one note at a time. All synthesisers place a limit on how many voices of polyphony are available. General-MIDI-compliant synthesisers are required to provide 24 voices of polyphony.

polyphony

The number of voices (notes) that a device can produce at once.

poly(phonic) pressure

Also called key pressure. A type of MIDI channel message by which each key senses and transmits pressure data independently.

pop shield/filter

A device placed over a microphone or between the microphone and singer to prevent loud popping sounds – caused by breath on the microphone – from being picked up.

port

1. An opening in a speaker case or just behind the diaphragm in a microphone casing. 2. A jack that accepts or sends digital data.

portamento

1. A pitch change that glides smoothly from one pitch to another. 2. The synthesiser mode or MIDI command that allows or causes this to happen.

ported-case microphone

A microphone with at least one port (opening behind the diaphragm) in its casing.

post-echo

The positioning of an echo send control after the main channel fader.

post-production

Production carried out after a film or video has been shot, including the recording of replacement dialogue, the addition of sound effects and the mixing of dialogue, effects and music.

pot

Abbreviation of *potentiometer*, a device that outputs part of the input voltage according to the position of the control's knob.

pre-amp

A low-noise amplifier designed to take a low-level signal and bring it up to normal line level.

precedence effect

A factor in human hearing where delay has a much bigger effect on the human perception of the location of the sound source than level does.

pre-delay

Delay circuits at the input of a reverb device that produce a delay before the reverberation is heard.

pre-echo

1. A repeating of the sound before the reverberation is heard. Used to simulate reflections found in a stage environment. 2. In tape recording, a low-level leakage of sound coming later, caused by print-through (ie data leaking through onto the other side of the tape). 3. In disc recording, a similar sound caused by a groove deforming a later groove. 4. The positioning of an echo send control before the main channel fader.

pre-emphasis

A boosting of high frequencies during the recording process in order to keep the signal above the level of noise at high frequencies.

pre-fader

The positioning of a send or other control before the main channel fader.

pre-fader listen

A solo circuit that allows a channel signal to be heard (and often metered) before the channel fader.

pre-mix

1. The same as *pong* (ie to play several recorded tacks with sync playback through a console in order to mix them together and record them on an open track). 2. To mix together the audio of several devices before sending the composite mix to the main console. 3. The composite mix of definitions 1 or 2.

pre-/post-switch

A switch on an input module which determines whether the echo send control comes before or after the main channel fader.

presence

The quality in an instrument (or sound source) that makes it sound like it's right there next to you.

presence frequencies

The range of audio frequencies between 4kHz and 6kHz that often, when boosted, increase the sense of presence, especially with voices.

pressure-gradient microphone

A microphone whose diaphragm is exposed at the front and at the back and whose diaphragm movement is caused by the difference in pressure between its front and back.

pressure microphone

A microphone whose diaphragm moves because the pressure of a sound wave causes one side of the diaphragm to work against the normal or controlled air pressure inside the mic case.

pressure-operated microphone

The same as *pressure microphone*.

pressure sensitivity

The feature in a synthesiser or keyboard controller of aftertouch (a control or operational function of a synthesiser where the exerting of pressure on a key after it has been pressed, and before it is released, will activate a control command that can be set by the player).

pressure zone microphone (PZM)

Barrier microphone manufactured by Crown. The head of the microphone is attached closely to a plate designed to be attached to a larger surface and which has a half-omni pick-up pattern.

processing

1. Function carried out by a computer performing its tasks as programmed. 2. Short for *signal processing*, ie changing the sound of an instrument or other sound source with equalisers, limiters, compressors or other devices and thereby "processing" them to be recorded onto a master.

processor

The part of a computer that actually performs task and calculations.

producer

The director of an audio-recording project and the person responsible for obtaining a final product of desired quality within a budget.

production

1. The recording of a tune, collection of tunes, video or film performance. 2. The action of directing an audio recording project to obtain a final product of desired quality within a budget.

program change

A MIDI message sent to a receiving device that will change its presets, causing a synthesiser or other device to switch to a new program (also called a preset or patch) contained in its memory.

program equalisation

Changing the level of any signal in a certain range of frequencies to emphasise or de-emphasise certain elements in the frequency of an instrument or sound source and change its tone.

programmable

A device – especially a computer-controlled device – is described as programmable if its parameters can be changed by the user.

program mode

An operational mode of a monitor section of a console where the monitor inputs are connected to the console outputs feeding the multitrack tape machine (used during a recording session).

program switch

A switch that activates the Program mode (Record mode) of the monitor section connecting the monitor inputs to the console outputs feeding the multitrack tape recorder (used during the recording session).

program time

In DAT recording, the time indication from the top of one selection.

prompt

A set of instructions that appear on a computer screen as a guide for the user to follow.

proprietary

Describing a function, feature or characteristic owned by one company and available only in units manufactured by that company.

proximity effect

In directional microphones, this is the boost in the microphone's output for bass frequencies as the mic is moved closer to the sound source.

psychoacoustics

The study of how things sound to individuals because of mental or emotional factors.

puck

Any circular piece of metal, fibre, rubber, etc, which drives something from a rotating power source.

pulse

A rise and then fall in amplitude, similar to a square wave, but one which stays up for less time than it stays down.

pulse-code modulation

The use of amplitude pulses in magnetic tape to record the digital information bits of digital audio.

pulse-wave modulation

Moving smoothly from a square wave to a pulse wave, in response to a control-voltage input (usually from a LFO).

pulse width

The amount of time that a pulse is at maximum voltage.

pumping breathing

The sound of noise changing volume as a limiter or compressor operates.

punching in

Putting a recorder/sequencer in Record mode on a previously recorded track while the track is playing in Sync Playback mode and the singer or musician is singing or playing along.

pure tone

A tone without harmonic frequencies (except for the fundamental frequency) and with a sine-wave shape.

PZM

A trademark belonging to Crown for its barrier microphone. (See *pressure zone microphone.*)

Q

The sharpness of the peak response in an equalisation circuit.

quality factor

The ratio of reactance to resistance in a coil which affects Q.

quantisation distortion/error

A modulation noise (also perceived as a distortion) that occurs in digital processing and recording and is caused by the sample levels being altered to conform to standard quantization levels.

quantisation levels/increments

A standard level that can be recognised by a digital recording system.

quantisation noise

A modulation noise (also perceived as distortion) that occurs in digital processing and recording and is caused by the sample levels being altered to conform to standard quantization levels. This is one of the types of error introduced into an analogue audio signal by encoding it in digital form. The digital equivalent of tape hiss, quantization noise is caused by the small differences between the actual amplitudes of the points being sampled and the bit resolution of the analogue-to-digital converter.

quantising

The conversion of the values of an analogue wave or random occurrence into steps. Quantizing is a function found on sequencers and drum machines and causes notes played at odd times to be "rounded off" to regular rhythmic values.

rack

1. The physical setting of a head in the direction toward or away from the tape, therefore affecting how much pressure is applied on the head by the tape. 2. Short for *equipment rack*, a cabinet with rails, or free-standing rails, that have holes in them to accept screws at standard spaces. Used to house outboard gear.

rack ears/flanges

Mounting brackets that can be attached to equipment to allow it to be housed in a standard equipment rack.

radiation

The angle and pattern of a speaker's coverage.

radiation pattern

A polar graph of the coverage of a speaker.

radio frequencies

Frequencies higher than 20kHz (usually above 100kHz).

ramp wave

A waveform that is similar to a sawtooth waveform but differs in that it starts at zero level and gradually rises to its peak level and then instantly drops back to zero level to form one cycle.

random-note generator

A device that generates unpredictable pitches at a set rate. Used in synthesisers.

random phase

The presence of many signals or reflections where some of the signals are in phase and some out of phase. The overall effect is that of being between in phase and out of phase.

rarefaction

The spreading apart of air particles in the formation of a sound-pressure wave.

rated load impedance

The input impedance (ie the opposition to current flow by a device's input) that a piece of equipment is designed to feed.

R-DAT

Abbreviation of *rotating-head digital audio tape*, a standard format for the recording of digital audio. Comprises a very small tape cassette and the recording process employs a rotating head.

recording chain

All of the transducers and changes of energy form in a recording and reproducing system listed in order.

recording solo

A switch or function which routes the signal of a channel to the monitor system by itself, and yet the signals out of the console to the recorder are uninterrupted.

reference level

1. A standard value used to describe the amount of level present in decibels above or below this reference. 2. The same as *operating level* (ie the maximum average level, which should not be exceeded in normal operation).

reflected sound

Sound that reaches a mic or listener after reflecting once or more from surrounding surfaces.

regeneration

1. The same as *jam sync*, ie a generation of a new SMPTE time-code signal according to the input SMPTE signal, giving an identical SMPTE signal out as the one that came in. 2. Feedback, especially around a delay line.

release

1. The rate at which the volume of a synthesiser drops to silence once a key is released. 2. The portion of an envelope that begins after a key is lifted.

release time

The time it takes for a dynamics-processing device to change gain when the input signal crosses the threshold level while decreasing.

release velocity

The speed with which a key is raised and the type of MIDI data used to encode that speed. Release-velocity sensing is found on some instruments, although it is rare. It's usually used to control the rate of the release segments of an envelope or envelopes.

repeat echo

An echo effect caused by discrete repetitions of a program source by using a long delay time and feedback on a delay line. Also called *space echo*.

resonance

1. The prolonging of a sound at a certain frequency and the tendency of something to vibrate at a particular frequency after the source of energy is removed. 2. A function on a filter in which a narrow band of frequencies (the resonance peak) becomes relatively more prominent. If the resonance peak is high enough, the filter will begin to oscillate and produce an audio output, even in the absence of input. Filter resonance is also known as *emphasis and Q*, and on some older instruments is also known as *regeneration* or *feedback* (because feedback was used in the circuit to produce a resonance peak).

resonant

1. Term used to describe equipment that tends to pass signals of a certain frequency or narrow range of frequencies more than signals of other frequencies. 2. Physical properties that tend to reinforce the energy at certain frequencies of vibration are described as being resonant.

resonant frequency

The frequency at which a physical item tends to vibrate after the source of energy (which causes the vibration) is removed.

resonate

1. To vibrate at the resonant frequency. 2. To linger on, as in reverberation. In this respect, the term is used in terms of sound in a room or is used to describe a room or other area that produces reverberation with a long reverb time.

return

Short for *echo return* or *auxiliary return*, ie the input of a console which brings the effect signal back from an echo chamber or other reverberation device.

reverb

1. The persistence of a sound after the source stops emitting it. 2. A function on a filter in which a narrow band of frequencies (the resonance peak) becomes relatively more prominent. If the resonance peak is high enough, the filter will begin to oscillate and produce an audio output, even in the absence of input. Filter resonance is also known as *emphasis and Q*, and on some older instruments is also known as *regeneration* or *feedback* (because feedback was used in the circuit to produce a resonance peak).

reverb(eration) time

The time it takes for the reverberation or echoes of a sound source to decrease by 60dB after the direct sound from the source stops.

reverberant field

The area away from a sound source at which reverberation is louder than the direct sound from the sound source.

reverberant field

The area, away from a sound source, where reverberation is louder than the direct sound from the sound source.

reverberation envelope

Literally, the attack, decay, sustain and release of the reverberation volume. In other words, the time it takes for the reverberation to reach its peak level and its rate of decay. (See also *ADSR*.)

RF

Abbreviation of *radio frequencies*, ie frequencies higher than 20kHz (usually above 100kHz).

RF interference

The induction of RF signals (usually broadcast by television and radio stations) into audio lines causing noise, buzzing and static.

ribbon microphone

A microphone with a thin, conductive ribbon as both the diaphragm and the generating element (the device that generates the electricity).

riding the faders

Moving a desk's faders up during quiet passages so that the signal will be recorded well above the noise and taking the faders back down during loud passages in order to prevent distortion.

ringing

An undesirable resonance at the cut-off frequency of a filter that has a high rate of cut-off.

ring modulator

A special type of mixer that accepts two signals as audio inputs and produces their sum-and-difference tones at its output but doesn't pass on the frequencies found in the original signals themselves. (See *clangorous*.)

rise time

The time it takes for an audio waveform to jump suddenly to a higher level.

RMS

Abbreviation of *root mean square*, the effective average value of an AC waveform.

roll-off

The reduction of signal level as a signal's frequency moves away from the cut-off frequency, especially when the cut-off rate is mild.

room EQ

An equaliser inserted in a monitor system that attempts to compensate for changes in frequency response caused by the acoustics of a room.

room sound

The ambience of a room, including reverberation and background noise.

room tone

The background noise in a room where there are no people speaking and there is no music playing.

round sound

A pleasingly balanced sound, ie one that has a pleasing mixture of high-frequency to low-frequency content.

rumble

A low-frequency noise, especially that caused by earth/floor vibration or by uneven surfaces in the drive mechanism of a recorder or playback unit.

run

In computer terminology, the term to run is applied to the performing of a function or command.

run-off

A quick reference mix recorded on cassette or some other format after a multitrack recording or overdubbing session so that the client can listen to what was recorded.

run through

Musicians run through a tune before the recording process begins so that the engineer can calibrate levels and check the sound quality.

sample and hold

1. In digital recording, a term used to describe the measuring of the level of a waveform at a given instant and then converting it to a voltage at that level, which will then be held until

another sample is taken. When triggered (usually by a clock pulse), a circuit on an analogue synthesiser looks at (samples) the voltage at its input and then passes it on to its output unchanged, regardless of what the input voltage does in the meantime (the hold period), until the next trigger is received. In one familiar application, the input was a noise source and the output was connected to oscillator pitch, which caused the pitch to change in a random staircase pattern. The sample-and-hold effect is often emulated by digital synthesisers through an LFO waveshape called "random".

sample dump

The copying of a digitally recorded sample without converting it to analogue between different storage units or sound modules through a MIDI transmission.

sample rate

In digital recording, this refers to the number of times that samples are taken each second.

sample-rate conversion

The conversion of digital audio data at one sample rate to digital audio data at a different sample rate without first converting the signal to analogue.

sampling frequency

The same as *sample rate*, ie the number samples taken each second. Typical sampling rates are usually between 11kHz and 48kHz.

sampling synchronisation signal

A stream of synchronisation pulses that are generated by a digital audio tape recorder, recorded onto tape and then used as a clock signal to time the sampling of the sampling circuits.

saturation

The point at which the tape is fully magnetised and will accept no more magnetisation.

sawtooth waveform

A waveform that jumps from a zero value to a peak value and then gradually diminishes to a zero value to complete the cycle.

SCSI

Abbreviation of *small-computer systems interface*, a high-speed communications protocol that allows computers, samplers and disk drives to communicate with one another. Pronounced "scuzzy".

SDII

Abbreviation of *Sound Designer II*, an audio file format and the native format of Digidesign's Sound Designer II graphic audio waveform editing program for the Macintosh.

SDS

The standard MIDI sample dump. SDS is used to transfer digital audio samples from one instrument to another over a MIDI cable.

sequence

1. An automatic playing of musical events (such as pitches, sounding of samples and rests) by a device in a step-by-step order. 2. The action of programming a computer to play musical events automatically, in a stepped order.

sequencer

1. A computer which can be programmed to play and record a stepped order of musical events. 2. A device or program that records and plays back user-determined sets of music-performance commands, usually in the form of MIDI data. Most sequencers also allow this data to be edited in various ways and stored on disk.

serial data

Digital data where all of the bits are transmitted one after another over a single wire or connection.

serial interface

A plug and cable for a computer that sends and receives data one bit after the other.

servo control

A motor used in a control circuit where the actual speed of the motor is sensed and compared to a reference, such as a pulse timing signal.

shelf

The frequency response of an equalisation circuit where the boost or cut-off frequencies form a shelf on a frequency response graph. A high-frequency shelf control will affect signal levels at the set frequency and all higher frequencies, while a low-frequency shelf control will affect signal levels at the set frequency and at all lower frequencies.

shelf filter

The circuit in an equaliser used to obtain the shelf.

shortest digital path

The routing of a digital-audio signal so that there is a minimum amount of digital-to-analogue, analogue-to-digital or sample-rate conversion.

shortest path

A technique in recording by which a signal is routed through the least amount of active (amplified) devices during recording.

shotgun microphone

A microphone with a long line filter (a tube that acoustically cancels sound arriving from the side), thus allowing the microphone to pick up sound in one direction much better than in any other direction.

shuttle

1. A technique used in older tape machines of stopping the fast winding (either fast-forward or rewind) of tape in older tape machines, where the engineer would put the tape machine in the opposite fast mode and press stop after the machine had just started to reverse direction. 2. Moving reels of a tape machine by hand so that the tape moves past the desired point first in one direction and then in the other, back and forth. 3. A control that moves the sound track either forward or backward when the control is moved off a centre point, either left or right.

sibilance

Energy from a voice centred at around 7kHz, caused by pronouncing "s", "sh" or "ch" sounds.

sidebands

Frequency components outside the natural harmonic series, generally introduced to a tone by using an audio-range wave for modulation. (See *clangorous*.)

signal

1. In audio, an alternating current or voltage matching the waveform of, or being originally obtained from, a sound-pressure wave. 2. In audio, an alternating current or voltage between 20Hz and 20kHz. 3. A digital-audio bit stream.

signal flow

The path that a signal follows through an audio system, such as a console.

signal generator

The same as *audio oscillator*, a device which emits test tones at various frequencies.

signal path

The way in which current travels or may travel across a circuit or through a device.

signal processing

Changing the sound of an instrument or some other sound source with equalisers, limiters, compressors and other devices, thereby "processing" the sound ready to be recorded onto a master.

signal-to-error ratio

The difference in level between the signal and the noise and distortion caused by converting analogue audio signals into digital audio and then back into analogue.

signal-to-noise ratio

The difference in decibels between the levels of signal and noise.

sine wave

The waveform produced by a sound source vibrating at just one frequency (ie making a pure tone).

single-D

Abbreviation of *single port distance*, used to describe a microphone in which there is one distance between the port and the diaphragm.

single-step mode

A method of loading events (such as notes) into memory one event at a time. Also called *step mode* and *step time*, compared with real time.

slap echo

One distinct repeat added to one or more instrument sounds in a mix that creates a very live sound, similar to what you'd hear in an arena.

slate

1. The voice recorded onto the beginning of a master tape to identify the tune and take, or the action of making it. 2. The circuit or control that allows you to slate masters.

slave

The transport that adjusts speed so that it's in time with the master transport when two machines are synced together.

slide

A control that has a knob which moves in a straight line and which outputs part of an input voltage according to the position of the knob.

smart FSK

An FSK (Frequency Shift Key) sync signal where the beginning of each measure has an identification message giving the measure number.

SMDI

Abbreviation of *SCSI musical data interchange*, a specification for sending MIDI sample dumps over the SCSI bus.

SMPTE

1. Society of Motion Picture and Television Engineers, a professional society. 2. A term loosely

used to mean *SMPTE time code*, a standardised timing and sync signal specified by the aforementioned society.

SND

Sound resource, a Macintosh audio file format.

Soft Knee

Generic name for the DBX Corporation's registered trade name of Over-Easy, named for the gradual change of compression ratio around the threshold, which makes it difficult to detect when compression is taking place.

song position pointer

1. Short for *MIDI clock with song pointer*, ie the time data contained in the MIDI signal used to sync two sequencers together. The song position pointer advances one step each $1/_{24}$ of a beat, and also has a number signal for each measure or bar which indicates the number of measures or bars you are into the tune. 2. A type of MIDI data that tells a device how many 16th-notes have passed since the beginning of a song. An SPP message is generally sent in conjunction with a MIDI Continue message in order to start playback from the middle of a song.

sostenuto pedal

A pedal found on grand pianos and mimicked on some synthesisers, which only sustain notes if they are already being held down on the keyboard at the moment when the pedal is pressed.

sound

1. Moving pressure variations in air caused by something vibrating between 20 times and 20,000 times a second, or similar variations in other substances, like water. 2. Loosely, any audio signal, regardless of its energy form.

sound absorption

The same as *acoustical absorption*, ie the quality of a surface or substance which takes in a sound wave rather than reflecting it.

sound file (soundfile)

A digital-audio recording that can be stored in a computer or on a digital storage medium, such as a hard disk.

sound-level meter

A device that measures sound-pressure levels.

sound module

The signal-generator portion of a synthesiser or a sample playback unit that sends out an audio signal according to incoming MIDI messages and does not have keys with which to be played.

sound-pressure level (SPL)

A measure of the sound pressure present, measured in decibels above the threshold of hearing (.0002 microbars).

sound-pressure wave

Alternate compressions (compacting together) and rarefactions (spreading apart) of air particles moving away from something that is vibrating at between 20 and 20,000 times a second, or a similar occurrence in another substance, such as water.

SoundTools

Digidesign's digital-audio-editing system.

soundtrack

An audio recording, especially on film or videotape.

sound wave

Abbreviation of *sound-pressure wave*, ie a wave of pressure changes moving away from something that is vibrating between 20 and 20,000 times a second.

source

Input mode on a tape machine/computer sequencer where the meters and the output of the machine's electronics will be the signal arriving at the input connector.

spaced cardioid pair

A far-distant miking technique of placing two cardioid microphones a distance apart (usually about six inches) and pointing away from each other by 90°.

spaced omni pair

Placing two microphones with omni-directional patterns between four and eight feet apart, so that one microphone picks up sound coming from the left and the other from the right.

spaced pair

Any two microphones spaced apart to obtain a stereo pick-up, especially using the spaced omni or spaced cardioid techniques.

space echo

An effect of repeating echoes of a sound.

SPDIF

Shortened from the first letters of Sony/Philips Digital Interface, a standard for sending and receiving digital audio signals using the common RCA connector.

speed of sound

The wave velocity (ie the time it takes for one point of the waveform to travel a certain distance) of a sound-pressure wave (1,130 feet per second at 70° Fahrenheit).

spin control

A British term for *feedback control*, ie a control that determines the amount of delayed signal sent back to the input of a delay line, used to produce repeated echo effects.

SPL

Abbreviation of *sound-pressure level*, referring to a pressure of .0002 microbars, considered to be the threshold of hearing (ie the lowest level at which people begin to hear sound).

splice

1. To assemble previously cut pieces of recording tape with special tape stuck on the back side.
2. An edit performed in this way.

splicing block

A device that holds recording tape to facilitate the cutting of splices.

spring reverb

A device that simulates reverberation by driving a spring (in the same way that a loudspeaker cone is driven) and picking up the spring's vibrations with a contact microphone (a device that converts physical vibrations into audio signals).

square wave

A wave shape produced when voltage rises instantly to one level, stays at that level, instantly falls to another level and stays at that level, and finally rises back to its original level to complete the cycle.

standard operating level

An operating level (ie the maximum average level that should not be exceeded in normal operation) that is widely used or widely referred to.

standing wave

An acoustic signal between two reflective surfaces with a distance that is an even multiple of half of the signal's frequency wavelength.

step input

In sequencing, a technique that allows you to enter notes one step at a time, also called *step recording*. Common step values are 16th- and eighth-notes. After each entry, the sequencer's clock (ie its position in the sequence) will advance one step and then stop, awaiting new input. Recording while the clock is running is called *real-time input*.

step program/mode/time

To program a sequencer one note (or event) at a time in accordance with the rhythm to which the time value of one step is set.

strike

To put away equipment and clean up after a session.

subcode

Control information bits that are recorded along with digital audio and can be used for control of the playback deck, including functions such as program numbers, start IDs and skip IDs.

subframe

A unit smaller than one frame in SMPTE time code.

submaster

The fader that controls the level of sound from several channels (although not usually all channels) during mixdown or recording.

submaster assignment

The selection of which bus (and therefore which submaster) the console channel will feed into, usually accomplished by pressing a button in the switch matrix.

submix

A combination of audio signals treated as one or two channels (to obtain a stereo image) in a mix.

subtractive synthesis

The generation of harmonically rich waveforms by various methods and then the filtering of these waveforms in order to remove unwanted harmonics and thus create sound. Alternatively, the technique of arriving at a desired tone colour by filtering waveforms rich in harmonics. Subtractive synthesis is the type generally used on analogue synthesisers.

sum

A signal comprising a combination of two stereo channels that are both equal in level and in phase.

sum and difference signals

When two stereo channels are mixed at equal levels and in phase, a sum signal is created. A difference signal is one where the mixture of the signals from the two channels has one channel phase-reversed so that any signal exactly the same in both channels will be cancelled.

surround sound

A technique of recording and playing back sound used in film, where the sound has a front-to-back quality as well as a side-to-side perspective.

sustain

1. A holding-out of the sounding of a pitch by an instrument. 2. The level at which a sound will continue to play when a synthesiser key is held down.

sweetening

Musical parts that are overdubbed in order to complete the music of a recording, especially the melodic instruments, such as strings and horns.

switch

A device that makes and/or breaks electrical connections.

switchable-pattern microphone

A microphone that has more than one directional pattern, depending on the position of the Pattern switch.

switch matrix

A series of switches – usually arranged in rows and columns of buttons – that allow any input module to be connected to any output bus.

sync

1. The circuits in a multitrack tape recorder which allow the record head to be used as a playback head for those tracks already recorded. 2. The same as *synchronisation*.

sync box

A device that takes several different kinds of sync signals and puts out several kinds of sync signal, allowing a device such as a sequencer to be driven by a sync signal that it doesn't recognise.

synchronisation

The running of two devices in time with each other so that the events generated by each of them will always fall into predicable time relationships.

sync word bits

A series of bits in SMPTE time code that identify the end of a frame.

system common

A type of MIDI data used to control certain aspects of the operation of an entire MIDI system.

System-common messages include Song Position Pointer messages, as well as Song Select, Tune Request, and End Of System Exclusive messages.

system exclusive (sysex)

A type of MIDI data that allows messages to be sent over a MIDI cable, which will then be responded to only by devices of a specific type. Sysex data is used most commonly for sending patch parameter data to and from an editor/librarian program.

system-exclusive bulk dump

A system-exclusive bulk dump is the transmission of internal synthesiser settings as a manufacturer-specified system-exclusive file from a synth to a sequencer or from a sequencer to a synth.

system real time

A type of MIDI data used for timing references. Because of its timing-critical nature, a system real-time byte can be inserted into the middle of any multibyte MIDI message. System real-time messages include MIDI Clock, Start, Stop, Continue, Active Sensing, and System Reset messages.

take notation

The noting down of the takes of a tune on a take sheet or track log, along with comments.

take sheet

A sheet used to note the number of takes made on each tune, along with comments.

talk box

A guitar effects unit that allows a voice to modulate (control) a guitar signal. Operated by a vocalist talking with a tube in his mouth.

tempo

The rate at which the music progresses, measured in beats per minute (ie the number of steady, even pulses that occur in each minute of the music).

tempo mapping

Programming a sequencer to follow the tempo variations of a recorded performance.

terminal

1. A point of connection between two wires, including a device on the end of a wire or cable that allows attachment and the accepting point on equipment casings. 2. A computer keyboard and monitor that allows access and entry of information into or from a computer.

THD

Abbreviation for *Total Harmonic Distortion*, an audio measurement specification used to determine the accuracy with which a device can reproduce an input signal at its output. THD describes the cumulative level of harmonic overtones that the device being tested adds to an input sine wave. THD + n is a specification that includes both harmonic distortion of the sine wave and non-harmonic noise.

thin sound

A sound that doesn't have all frequencies present. Especially refers to a sound deficient in low frequencies.

three-to-one rule

The rule which states that the distance between microphones must be at least three times the distance between either microphone and the sound source.

three-way speaker

A speaker system with separate speakers to reproduce the bass, mid-range and treble frequencies.

threshold

The level at which a dynamics-processing unit begins to change gain.

threshold control

The control on a dynamics-processing device that adjusts the threshold level (ie the level at which it begins to change gain).

threshold of feeling

The sound-pressure level at which people experience discomfort for 50 per cent of the time.

threshold of hearing

The sound-pressure level at which people can hear for only 50 per cent of the time.

threshold of pain

The sound-pressure level at which people feel actual pain for 50 per cent of the time.

thru box

A unit with one MIDI In port and several MIDI Out ports. Each MIDI Out port has the same signal as the MIDI In port, but with a delay of the signal (usually around 4ms).

thru port

A connector that puts out a MIDI signal identical to the input MIDI signal.

tie lines

Cables with connectors at both ends so that a signal can be sent or picked up from a remote location. Usually run through walls or floors.

tight/hyped sound

The sound obtained by close-miking well-isolated instruments.

timbre

1. The timbre of the instrument is what makes it sound like that particular instrument and not like any other, even though the other instrument may be playing the same pitch. 2. One of the building blocks of a patch in a Roland synthesiser. Pronounced "tam-br".

time base

The number of pulses/advances per beat in a simple clock signal.

time code

Short for *SMPTE time code*, a standardised timing and sync signal specified by the Society of Motion Picture and Television Engineers. Alternatively, a type of signal that contains information about location in time and used for a synchronisation reference point when synchronising two or more machines together, such as sequencers, drum machines and tape decks.

time-code generator

A unit that generates SMPTE time-code signals.

time compression/expansion

The speeding up or slowing down of an audio recording without changing the pitch.

time constant

In a circuit that has reactance, the time it takes for the current or voltage to substantially stabilise in the circuit when the voltage or current is changing.

timing clock

1. An even pulse signal used for syncing purposes. 2. The same as MIDI Clock, ie time data in a MIDI signal that advances one step each $^{1}/_{24}$ of a beat and can be used to sync two sequencers together.

timing tape

Plastic leader tape with marks every 7.5 inches along it. Used to edit silence between selections.

tiny telephone jack/plug

A smaller version of the phone jack/plug (ie .173 inches in diameter, rather than .25 inches) used in many patch bays.

tone

1. One of several single-frequency signals found at the beginning of a tape reel at the magnetic reference level that will be used to record a program. 2. Any single-frequency signal or sound. 3. The sound quality of an instrument's sound relative to the amount of energy present at different frequencies. 4. In some synthesisers, a term meaning the audio signal that will be put out by the unit which would be similar to the sound of an instrument.

touch sensitive

Used to describe a synthesiser keyboard's ability to generate a MIDI Velocity signal. Not all synthesiser keyboards are touch sensitive.

tracking

Recording the individual tracks of a multitrack recording.

transducer

A device that converts energy from one medium to another.

transfer curve

A graph of energy supplied versus energy stored by a storage medium (often magnetic tape).

transformer

An electrical device that has two magnetically coupled coils.

transformer matrix

A device that uses transformers to take two audio channel inputs and change them to a sum signal (ie a mix of the signals on the two channels) and a difference signal (ie the mixture of the two signals with the phase of one channel reversed so that any signal exactly the same in both channels will be cancelled).

transient

The initial high-energy peak that occurs at the beginning of a waveform, such as one caused by the percussive action of a pick or hammer hitting a string.

transient response

Response to signals with amplitudes which rise very quickly, such as drumbeats and waveforms produced by percussive instruments.

transpose

The act of changing the musical register of an entire piece of music by the space of an interval.

trap

A filter designed to reject audio signals at certain frequencies.

triangular wave

A waveform that looks triangular.

trigger

1. The signal or action of sending a signal to control the start of an event. 2. A device that emits a signal to control the start of an event, including a device that puts out such a signal when struck.

trim

1. Abbreviation of *trim control*. 2. To make a small adjustment to any control.

trim control

A device that reduces the strength of a signal produced by an amplifier, often over a restricted range.

trim status

Solid State Logic's Console Automation mode, which operates as follows: when a slide is at its trim point, the gain variations (fader movements) last programmed in the computer will be in effect; when the slide is moved from the trim point, gain or loss is added to or subtracted from the program.

truncation

The editing of a sample playback so that only the desired portion of the sample is played. Effected by moving the start and end points of the sample playback.

tube

An abbreviation of *vacuum tube*, ie an amplifying device that has elements to send and control current through a vacuum in a glass or metal tube.

tuned

A term used with reference to a circuit or device which is most sensitive to a certain frequency.

turnover frequency

The same as *cut-off frequency*, ie the highest or lowest frequency in the pass band of a filter.

tweeter

A speaker designed to reproduce only higher frequencies.

unbalanced

Used to describe a method of interconnecting recorders, amplifiers and other electronic gear using twin-conductor cable.

unidirectional

A pick-up pattern that is more sensitive to sound arriving from one direction than from any other.

unity gain

No increase or decrease in signal strength at the output of an amplifier or device when compared to the signal strength at the input.

vacuum tube

An amplifying device that has elements to send and control current through a vacuum in a glass or metal tube.

vamp

The repeated part of a tune at its end, usually the chorus or part of the chorus.

vamp and fade

A method of ending a recording of a tune where part of the music is repeated and the engineer reduces volume until the music fades out.

VCA

Abbreviation for *voltage-controlled amplifier*, ie an amplifier that will change gain according to the level of control voltage sent to it.

VCA automation

A system of channel gain (or other functions) controlled by a computer via the use of voltage-controlled amplifiers, which change gain according to the level of control voltages sent to them by the computer.

VCA fader

A fader with a VCA in its casing arranged so that, in manual operation, the slide of the fader controls how much control voltage is sent to the VCA and therefore controls the channel gain.

VCF

1. Abbreviation of *voltage-controlled filter*, the cut-off frequency of which can be changed by altering the amount of voltage being sent to its control input. 2. The digital equivalent of a VCF.

VCO

1. Abbreviation of *foltage-control oscillator*, which generates an AC control voltage, usually in the form of a low-frequency oscillator putting out a signal between .1Hz and 10Hz. 2. Abbreviation of *voltage-controlled oscillator*, which changes its frequency according to a

control voltage fed to its control input.

velocity

In synthesisers and keyboard controllers, a MIDI message giving data on how hard a key is struck. Alternatively, a type of MIDI data (ranging between 1 and 127) usually used to indicate how quickly a key is pushed down (attack velocity) or allowed to rise (release velocity). (A Note On message with a velocity value of zero is equivalent to a Note Off message.)

velocity curve

A map that translates incoming velocity values into other velocities in order to alter the feel or response of a keyboard or tone module.

velocity microphone

Another name for *pressure-gradient microphone* (ie a microphone whose diaphragm is exposed at the front and at the back and whose diaphragm movement is caused by the difference in pressure between its front and back).

vocoder

An effects device that will modulate (control) one signal with another.

voice stealing

A process by which a synthesiser that is being required to play more notes than it has available voices switches off some of the voices that are currently sounding (typically those that have been sounding the longest or are the lowest amplitude) in order to assign them to play new notes.

volatile memory

Computer memory that will be lost when the computer is turned off.

voltage-controlled amplifier

The same as *VCA*, ie an amp that changes gain according to the level of control voltage sent to it.

voltage-controlled attenuator

Similar to a voltage-controlled amplifier, except that, with no control voltage sent to it, the amplifier will have no gain and no loss. As an increasing control voltage is sent to it, the amplifier reduces gain, causing a loss of signal strength.

voltage-controlled fader

The same as *VCA fader* (ie a fader with a VCA in its casing arranged so that, in manual operation, the slide of the fader controls how much control voltage is sent to the VCA and therefore controls the channel gain).

voltage-controlled filter

A filter (especially a low-pass filter) that will change its cut-off frequency according to the level of the control voltage being fed to its control input.

voltage-control oscillator

The same as definition 2 of *VCO*, ie an oscillator that changes its frequency according to a control voltage fed to its control input.

vox

Latin for "voice", used on track logs to denote a vocal track.

VSO

Another term for a *vacuum-tube voltmeter*, ie a device that measures the electrical voltage and uses a vacuum tube to drive the indicator so that testing the circuit does not load the circuit.

VU

Abbreviation of term *volume unit* (a unit designed to measure changes in loudness in audio).

WAV

The Windows audio file format. Typically encountered as "filename.wav".

wave

A continuous fluctuation in the amplitude of a quantity with respect to time.

waveform

The shape made by fluctuations in a wave over a period over time.

wavelength

The length of one cycle (in feet, inches, etc) of a wave.

wavetable synthesis

A common method for generating sound electronically on a synthesiser or PC. Output is produced using a table of sound samples (actual recorded sounds) which are digitised and played back as needed. By continuously re-reading samples and looping them together at different pitches, highly complex tones can be generated from a minimum of stored data without overtaxing the processor.

wave velocity

The time it takes for one point of a waveform to travel a certain distance.

weighting

An equalisation curve used in audio tests that compensates for the Fletcher Munson effect at various levels.

wet

Having reverberation or ambience. Alternatively, consisting entirely of processed sound. The output of an effects device is 100 per cent wet when only the output of the processor itself is being heard, with none of the dry (unprocessed) signal.

white noise

Random energy distributed so that the amount of energy is the same for each cycle, causing the noise level to increase with frequency.

wide-band noise

Noise that has energy over a wide range of frequencies.

woofer

A speaker designed to reproduce only bass frequencies.

workstation

A device that controls a variety of functions and is designed to be operated by one person, comprising a synthesiser or sampler in which several of the tasks usually associated with electronic music production – such as sequencing, effects processing, rhythm programming and storing data on disk – can all be performed by components found within a single physical device.

wow

A low pitch change that occurs because the speed of a recorder or playback machine fluctuates slowly.

write mode

A mode of operation in an automated console where an engineer is in control of channel gain and the computer stores the changes in gain effected by the engineer over a period of time.

XLR connector

1. A common three-pin connector used in balanced audio connections. 2. A microphone cable.

XY miking

A method of arranged two cardioid microphones for stereo pick-up, with the two mic heads positioned as close together as possible without touching, pointing 90° away from each other and 45° to the centre of the sound source.

Y-cord/lead

A cable fitted with three connectors, so that one output may be sent to two inputs.

zenith

The tilt of the tape head in the direction perpendicular to the travel of the tape.

zero-crossing point

The point at which a digitally encoded waveform crosses the centre of its amplitude range.